Fathers

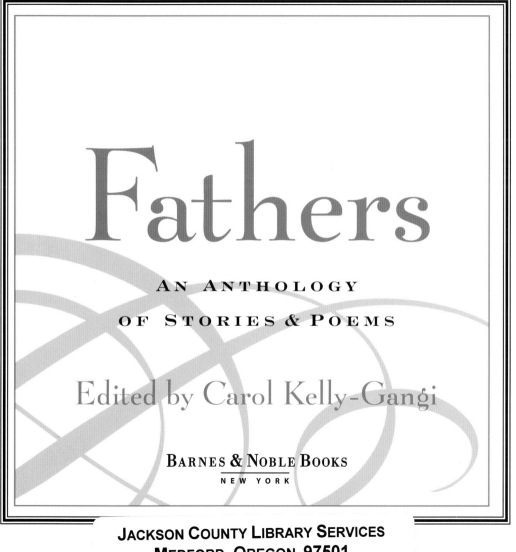

Fathers

AN ANTHOLOGY
OF STORIES & POEMS

Edited by Carol Kelly-Gangi

BARNES & NOBLE BOOKS
NEW YORK

"Shooting Dad" reprinted with the permission of Simon & Schuster Adult Publishing Group from TAKE THE CANNOLI by Sarah Vowell. Copyright © 2000 by Sarah Vowell.

Letter from F. Scott Fitzgerald reprinted with permission of Scribner, an imprint of Simon & Schuster Adult Publishing Group, from F. Scott Fitzgerald: A LIFE IN LETTERS, edited by Matthew J. Bruccoli. Copyright © 1994 by the Trustees under Agreement Dated July 3, 1975, created by Frances Scott Fitzgerald Smith.

Letter from Ogden Nash copyright © 1990 by Isabel Nash Eberstadt and Linell Nash Smith. Reprinted by permission of Curtis Brown, Ltd.

Photo Credits

© Corbis: pp. 2, 12, 17, 22, 29, 36, 58, 60, 105, 130, 144, 149, 151, 155, 160
© Getty Images: p; 76, 140

Compilation and introduction copyright © 2004 by Barnes & Noble, Inc.

2004 Barnes & Noble Books
ISBN 0-7607-5302-4
Book design by Leah Lococo Ltd
Printed and bound in China

To Dad with love and gratitude

Acknowledgments

I'D LIKE TO THANK Rick Campbell and Heather Russell-Revesz for the opportunity to compile this anthology. And loving thanks to my parents, Howard and Gwen Kelly, for their tireless love and support. A special thanks to my family, especially Barbara Kelly-Vergona, Marianne Kelly, Theresa Kelly, Lori Kelly, Beverly Lindh, Paul and Vivian Gangi, Paul E. Gangi, Joanne Gangi, Rose Stallmeyer, and Kristen Sheik, for all of their suggestions, support, and help with John Christopher. And, as always, to John for his love and for being the wonderful father that he is.

A special thanks to all of those who graciously allowed me to reprint their favorite recipes for Dads: Charlie Briganti, Vivian Gangi, Gwen Kelly, Beverly Lindh, Mary Perillo, John Petrella, George and Marlene Petrella, Kevin Rowson, Don Stefanelli, Tony Stefanelli, Jim Tavormina, Anthony Vergona, and to my twin sister, Barbara Kelly-Vergona for all of her efforts in compiling them.

Table of Contents

FAVORITE RECIPES FOR DAD

Introduction

∗⟨∞⟩∗

"I could not point to any need in childhood as strong as that for a father's protection." —SIGMUND FREUD

*T*HE RELATIONSHIP BETWEEN FATHER AND CHILD is one of biblical proportions. Far from being a mere substitute for mothers, what a father gives to a child is utterly unique and something that only he can give. In fact, many of today's fathers choose to do it all. That is to say, while there was a time when mothers and fathers inhabited very different spheres as far as parenting was concerned, many fathers now take an active role in the day-to-day care and nurturing of their children—usually after working a full day on the job.

Fathers is a book that is for and about these all-important figures. Each selection of prose and poetry explores some aspect of fatherhood. Some contributors offer deeply personal accounts of their relationships with their own fathers. In "My Father on the Verge of Disgrace," John Updike pens a narrative, both candid and bitter-sweet, revealing how his spirited father mortified him in his youth. Jimmy Carter relates an incident from his childhood where his father's forgiveness left him awe-inspired. In "From Father, with Love," Doris Kearns Goodwin lovingly recalls her dad and the lifelong passion for baseball that the two shared. And in "To My Father: What I've Never Said," Joyce Carol Oates writes eloquently of her father and of the selfless love that is parenting at its best.

Other contributors offer insights and incidents from their own experiences as fathers. Lafcadio Hearn and Christopher Morley describe the intense emotions evoked by the sight of their newborn children. Henry Wadsworth Longfellow celebrates his young daughters in his classic poem, "The Children's Hour." While in "Golden Time," Al Roker humorously describes the alternating joy and exhaustion that comes with parenting young children.

Still other writers focus on the father-child relationship—both richly simple and deeply complex. In "Simon's Papa," Guy de Maupassant pens a thoughtful tale about a young peasant boy's desperate search for a father. Whereas in "My Son the Murderer," Bernard Malamud writes poignantly of a father's helplessness as he watches his son slip into depression and despair during the Vietnam war.

Since advice—whether solicited or not—has always been an important part of fathering, it seemed only natural to include a selection of letters from fathers to their children. Charles Dickens and F. Scott Fitzgerald share with their children wise words on what is truly important in life; Ogden Nash lovingly cautions his daughter about the value of good morals; while Theodore Roosevelt extols the meaning of good character to his sons.

A tribute to dads everywhere, *Fathers* is a meant as a heartfelt thank-you to those men who shape our lives from the moment we are born and whose love and guidance cast a lasting impression on us for the rest of our lives.

—CAROL KELLY-GANGI, Rumson, New Jersey

PART I

New Fathers

When one becomes a father, then first one becomes a son. Standing by the crib of one's own baby, with that world-old pang of compassion and protectiveness toward this so little creature that has all its course to run, the heart flies back in yearning and gratitude to those who felt just so toward one's self. Then for the first time one understands the homely succession of sacrifices and pains by which life is transmitted and fostered down the stumbling generations of men.

—CHRISTOPHER MORLEY

The Rainbow

BY D. H. LAWRENCE

FROM THE FIRST, the baby stirred in the young father a deep, strong emotion he dared scarcely acknowledge, it was so strong and came out of the dark of him. When he heard the child cry, a terror possessed him, because of the answering echo from the unfathomed distances in himself. Must he know in himself such distances, perilous and imminent?

He had the infant in his arms, he walked backwards and forwards troubled by the crying of his own flesh and blood. This was his own flesh and blood crying! His soul rose against the voice suddenly breaking out from him, from the distances in him. . . .

He became accustomed to the child, he knew how to lift and balance the little body. The baby had a beautiful rounded head that moved him passionately. He would have fought to the last drop to defend that exquisite, perfect round head.

He learned to know the little hands and feet, the strange, unseeing, golden-brown eyes, the mouth that opened only to cry, or to suck, or to show a queer, toothless laugh. He could almost understand even the dangling legs, which at first had created in him a feeling of aversion. They could kick in their queer little way, they had their own softness.

One evening, suddenly, he saw the tiny, living thing rolling naked in the mother's lap, and he was sick, it was so utterly helpless and vulnerable and extraneous; in a world of hard surfaces and varying altitudes, it lay vulnerable and naked at every point. Yet it was quite blithe. And yet, in its blind, awful crying, was there not the blind, far-off terror of its own vulnerable nakedness, the terror of being so utterly delivered over, helpless at every point. He could not bear to hear it crying. His heart strained and stood on guard against the whole universe.

But he waited for the dread of these days to pass; he saw the joy coming. He saw the lovely, creamy, cool little ear of the baby, a bit of dark hair rubbed to a bronze floss, like bronze-dust. And he waited, for the child to become his, to look at him and answer him.

It had a separate being, but it was his own child. His flesh and blood vibrated to it. He caught the baby to his breast with his passionate, clapping laugh. And the infant knew him.

As the newly opened, newly dawned eyes looked at him, he wanted them to perceive him, to recognize him. Then he was verified. The child knew him, a queer contortion of laugher came on its face for him. He caught it to his breast, clapping with a triumphant laugh.

The golden-brown eyes of the child gradually lit up and dilated at the sight of the dark-glowing face of the youth. It knew its mother better, it wanted its mother more. But the brightest, sharpest little ecstasy was for the father.

It began to be strong, to move vigorously and freely, to make sounds like words. It was a baby girl now. Already it knew his strong hands, it exulted in his strong clasp, it laughed and crowed when he played with it.

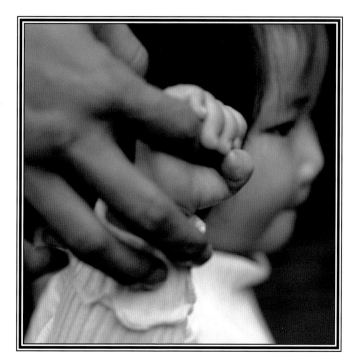

No man can possibly know what life means, what the world means, what anything means, until he has a child and loves it. And then the whole universe changes and nothing will ever again seem exactly as it seemed before.

—LAFCADIO HEARN

We think of a father as an old, or at least a middle-aged man. The astounding truth is that most fathers are young men, and that they make their greatest sacrifices in their youth. I never meet a young man in a public park on Sunday morning wheeling his first baby without feeling an ache of reverence. —JAMES DOUGLAS

Not long ago I fell in love,
　　But unreturned is my affection—
That girl that I'm enamored of
　　Pays little heed in my direction.

I thought I knew her fairly well:
　　In fact, I'd had my arm around her;
And so it's hard to have to tell
　　How unresponsive I have found her.

For, though she is not frankly rude,
　　Her manners quite the wrong way rub me:
It seems to me ingratitude
　　To let me love her—and then snub me!

Though I'm considerate and fond,
　　She shows no gladness when she spies me—
She gazes off somewhere beyond
　　And doesn't even recognize me.

Her eyes, so candid, calm and blue,
    Seem asking if I can support her
In the style appropriate to
    A lady like her father's daughter.

Well, if I can't, then no one can—
    And let me add that I intend to:
She'll never know another man
    So fit for her to be a friend to.

Not love me, eh? She better had!
    By Jove, I'll make her love me one day;
For, don't you see, I am her Dad,
    And she'll be three weeks old on Sunday!

—CHRISTOPHER MORLEY

PART II

Fathers and Children

To My Little Daughter

Across the grass I see her pass,
　　She walks with stately grace;
A winsome little brown-haired lass,
　　With rose-buds in her face.

Fairest of all fair flowers that grow—
　　A lily, pure and white;
The one fond treasure that I know,
　　Most perfect in my sight.

My every joy—I hold it true—
　　In you must find a part;
You are the sunlight breaking through
　　The winter of my heart.

—E. J. FRANCIS DAVIES

Don't Make Me Stop This Car!

BY AL ROKER

I LOVE MY DAUGHTERS. I cherish the time I get to spend with each of them. I have Courtney for a limited time each month, and that time is very special to me.

Because of my job, I'm not home during the week to see Leila wake up. I'm treated to those moments only on the weekend, and I enjoy every minute of it. I'm reminded of similar times I shared with Courtney almost thirteen years earlier. From the illuminating smile that greets me when I enter the room, to that all-powerful scent that greets me when I unsnap her onesie and pull the adhesive tabs off her Pamper.

But there is a time that every parent comes to appreciate. A special time that descends upon them after a long day when their precious bundle has been particularly trying or difficult. A time that you, as a parent, embrace and love. I call it "Golden Time."

What is Golden Time? It's the first five minutes after all the kids are asleep and you slump down in your favorite chair or couch and let out a long, deep breath. You savor the silence that has descended upon your abode. You drink in the quiet most of which you gladly traded the second that tiny person entered your life.

Obviously, the more children in your house, the harder it is to achieve Golden Time. My parents had six of us running around with a span of seventeen years between my baby brother and me. For them, Golden Time might not occur until ten or eleven at night. In fact, my father would just fall asleep waiting for Golden Time. Most nights he gave up on the whole concept and just went to bed.

My parents had to wait forty-four years for the ultimate Golden Time. That's when my youngest brother, Chris, got married and moved out of the house. Now their whole day is nothing but Golden Time. Well, for my mom, Golden Time occurs when Dad goes out fishing. And for Dad, it's when Mom goes out bowling. But the point is, it took them a loooooooong time.

In the beginning, it is very hard to reach Golden Time with a newborn. The problem is, you know that the child is going to wake up again pretty soon. The question is . . . when? An hour? Two hours? Fifteen minutes? Who knows? So you can't settle in, take that deep breath, let it out, and just relax. You are still in a state of full readiness. At any moment, the air-raid siren sleeping in the next room could go off and you have to hit the ground running. Breast, bottle, diaper, whatever he or she needs, you have to be ready to provide it.

No, Golden Time can be achieved only when your baby is sleeping for long intervals, thereby allowing you to sleep for long intervals. I remember the realization that Courtney was hitting her stride when it came to sleep. At the time, I was still working the eleven o'clock news and we lived about an hour north of New York City in Westchester.

By the time I got off the train, drove home, let the dog out, and hit the sack, it was about 1 A.M. Courtney timed it so that I would just be hitting my REM sleep stage when she woke up and demanded a bottle at 2 A.M. It worked out to an hour after I hit the pillow. If the news was late and I got to bed at, say, 2 A.M., she'd wake up at 3. It got to the point where I'd just bring the bottle with me and put it on the nightstand. An hour later, her bottle was the perfect temperature thereby saving me a trip back down to the kitchen.

Because of my schedule, I never achieved Golden Time with Courtney during the week. The weekend, however, was another story. Saturdays were what I called "Courtney-Daddy Day." Mommy had her all week, and needed a break to do frivolous things such as regain her sanity, get her hair done, talk to adults—silly activities that kept her from loading up the car and driving to points unknown.

For those of you who have toddlers, you know what I'm talking about. These tiny versions of us possess the power of speech, mobility, and limited reasoning. They can do just enough to make you crazy. They can't quite dress themselves, but they can tell you that they don't like what you've put them in. They don't like what you've made for lunch, but they don't know what they want. They can get inside the closet and wreck things, but they can't get out.

For most dads, the weekday world of child-raising consists of seeing your babies before you go to work, getting a dose of them before bedtime, and, if Mom is lucky, reading to them and then putting them to bed. The weekend is a concentrated dose of child-rearing and there is no letup. Don't get me wrong, I loved every minute of it with Courtney, but it was relentless.

It was then that I put a name to the feeling that washed over me when I would get her to bed on a Saturday night. It was a more intense version of the feeling that came over me when I had worked really hard that week. I got that paycheck and looked at the net income window and WOW!!! Golden Time!

As I sat in my chair, slowly recovering from the day, my baby asleep in her bed upstairs, that same sensation crept through my being. A sense of accomplishment from doing something you really loved, while at the same time being incredibly tired yet satisfied. Savoring what had transpired earlier, yet being glad it was over with for a little while.

These days, with Leila, Golden Time has taken on new meaning. Now that she's a year and a half, she is motoring from room to room, jabbering nonstop, and keeping Deborah and me on the run. I've extended the time I describe as Golden Time to include the time in the morning that Leila lets us lie in bed and just enjoy being a couple, able to talk about the day ahead and just be.

Suddenly a small voice pierces the silence, signaling that Golden Time is over. A different kind of Golden Time replaces it. Once again, just as with Courtney, a tiny face that lights up when it sees me poke my head in the room fills my heart with pure gold. Who needs Golden Time? All these moments are priceless.

The Children's Hour

Between the dark and the daylight,
　　When the night is beginning to lower,
Comes a pause in the day's occupations,
　　That is known as the Children's Hour.

I hear in the chamber above me
　　The patter of little feet,
The sound of a door that is opened,
　　And voices soft and sweet.

From my study I see in the lamplight,
　　Descending the broad hall stair,
Grave Alice, and laughing Allegra,
　　And Edith with golden hair.

A whisper, and then a silence:
　　Yet I know by their merry eyes
They are plotting and planning together
　　To take me by surprise.

A sudden rush from the stairway,
　　A sudden raid from the hall!
By three doors left unguarded
　　They enter my castle wall!

They climb up into my turret
    O'er the arms and back of my chair;
If I try to escape, they surround me;
    They seem to be everywhere.

They almost devour me with kisses,
    Their arms about me entwine,
Till I think of the Bishop of Bingen
    In his Mouse-Tower on the Rhine!

Do you think, O blue-eyed banditti,
    Because you have scaled the wall,
Such an old mustache as I am
    Is not a match for you all!

I have you fast in my fortress,
    And will not let you depart,
But put you down into the dungeon
    In the round-tower of my heart.

And there will I keep you forever,
    Yes, forever and a day,
Till the walls shall crumble to ruin,
    And moulder in dust away!

—HENRY WADSWORTH LONGFELLOW

Our Son

He's supposed to be our son, our hope and our pride,
In him all the dreams of our future abide,
But whenever some act to his credit occurs
I never am mentioned, the glory is hers,
And whenever he's bad or has strayed from the line,
Then always she speaks of the rascal as mine.

When trouble has come she will soberly say:
"Do you know what your son has been up to today?
Your son spilled the ink on the living-room floor!
Your son broke the glass in the dining-room door!
I am telling you now something has to be done,
It is high time you started correcting your son!"

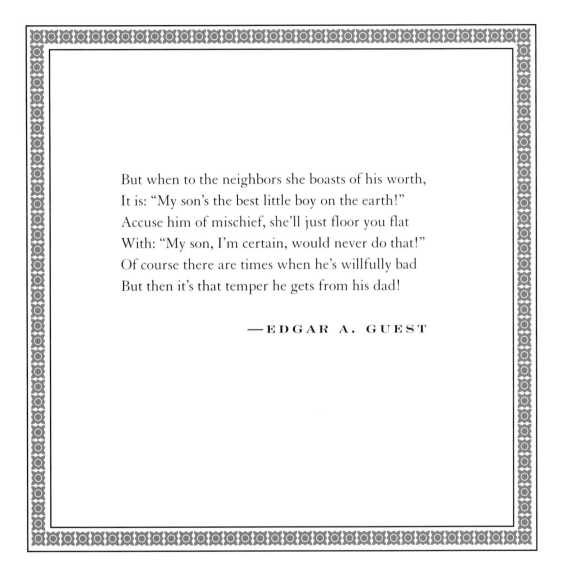

But when to the neighbors she boasts of his worth,
It is: "My son's the best little boy on the earth!"
Accuse him of mischief, she'll just floor you flat
With: "My son, I'm certain, would never do that!"
Of course there are times when he's willfully bad
But then it's that temper he gets from his dad!

—EDGAR A. GUEST

Boys and girls need chances to be around their father, to be enjoyed by him and if possible to do things with him. Better to play 15 minutes enjoyably and then say, "Now I'm going to read my paper" than to spend all day at the zoo crossly.

—DR. BENJAMIN SPOCK

When I was a boy of fourteen, my father was so ignorant I could hardly stand to have the old man around. But when I got to be twenty-one, I was astonished at how much he had learned in seven years.

—MARK TWAIN

My Father on the Verge of Disgrace

BY JOHN UPDIKE

$\mathcal{I}$T FILTERED even into my childhood dreams, the fear. The fear that my father would somehow fall from his precarious ledge of respectability, a ledge where we all stood with him. "We all"—his dependents, my mother, her parents, myself. The house we lived in was too big for us: my grandfather had bought it in 1922, when he felt prosperous enough to retire. Within the decade, the stock-market crash took all his savings. He sat in one corner of the big house, the little "sunroom" that looked toward the front yard, the hedge, and the street with its murmuring traffic. My grandmother, bent over and crippled by arthritis, hobbled about in the kitchen and out into the back yard, where she grew peas and kept chickens. My mother had her nook upstairs, at a little desk with wicker sides, where she did not like to be interrupted, and my father was generally out somewhere in the town. He was a tall, long-legged man who needed to keep moving. The year I was born, he had lost his job, as salesman in the mid-Atlantic territory for a line of quality English china. Only after three years—anxious years for him, but for me just the few buried smells and visions retained by my infant memory—did he succeed in getting another job, as a high-school teacher. It was as a schoolteacher that I always knew him. Wearing a suit, his shirt pocket holding a pack of cigarettes and a mechanical pencil and a fountain pen, he loomed to me as a person of eminence in the town; it was this sense of his height that led, perhaps, to my fear that he would somehow topple.

One of my dreams, borrowing some Depression imagery from the cartoons in the newspaper, had him clad in a barrel and, gray-faced, being harried down the Town Hall steps by the barking apparitions of local officialdom. The crowd began to throw things, and my attempt at explaining, at pleading for him, got caught in my throat. In this present day of strip malls and towns that are mere boundaries on a developer's map, it is hard to imagine the core of authority that existed then in small towns, at least in the view of a child—the power of righteousness and enforcement that radiated from the humorless miens of the central men. They were not necessarily officials; our town was too small to have many of those. And the police chief was a perky, comically small man who inspired fear in no one, not even in first-graders as he halted traffic to let them cross the street to the elementary school. But certain local merchants, a clergyman or two, the undertaker whose green-awninged mansion dominated the main intersection, across from a tavern and a drugstore, not to mention the druggist and the supervising principal of the school where my father taught, projected a potential for condemnation and banishment.

To have this power, you had to have been born in the town, or at least in the locality, and my father had not been. His accent, his assumptions were slightly different. This was Pennsylvania, and he was from New Jersey. My mother came from the area, and she may have married my father in hopes of escaping it. But the land of six decades ago had more gravity than it does now; it exerted a grip. Fate, or defeat, returned my parents to live in my grandfather's big house, a house where only I, growing up day by day, felt perfectly at home.

I was proud of my schoolteacher father. If his suit was out of press, and his necktie knotted awry, I was too new to the world to notice. He combed his hair back and, in the style of his generation, parted it near the middle. In our kitchen, he would bolt his orange juice (squeezed on one of those ribbed glass sombreros and then poured off through a strainer) and grab a bite of toast (the toaster a simple tin box, a kind of little hut with slit and slanted sides, that rested over a gas burner and browned one side of the bread, in stripes, at a time), and then he would dash, so hurriedly that his necktie flew back over his shoulder, down through our yard, past the grapevines hung with buzzing Japanese-beetle traps, to the yellow brick building, with its tall smokestack and wide playing fields, where he taught. Though the town had some hosiery and hat factories tucked around in its blocks of row houses, the high school was the most impressive building on my horizon. To me it was the center of the universe. I enjoyed the gleams of recognition that fell to me from my father's high visibility. His teaching colleagues greeted me on the street with a smile; other adults seemed to know me and included me in a sort of ironical forbearance. He was not a drinker—his anxious stomach was too tender for that—but he had the waywardly sociable habits of a drinker. He needed people, believed in their wisdom and largesse, as none of the rest of us who lived in the house did: four recluses and an extrovert. Imitating my mother, I early developed a capacity to entertain myself, with paper and the images it could be made to bear. When school—the elementary school, at the other end of town, along the main street—took me into its classes, I felt, in relation to my classmates, timid.

He called me "young America," as if I were more bumptious than I was. He pushed me about the town with a long stick he had made, whose fork gripped the back of my red wagon, so that all I had to do was sit in it and steer. No more births followed mine. My bedroom was a narrow back room, with a bookshelf and some framed illustrations, by Vernon Grant, of nursery rhymes. It overlooked the back yard and adjoined my parents' bedroom. I could hear them talk at night; even when the words were indistinct, the hiss of unhappiness, of obscure hot pressures, came through the walls. *"That son of a bitch,"* my father would say, of some man whose name I had missed. *"Out to get me,"* I would hear. Who could this enemy be, I would wonder, while my mother's higher, more rhythmic voice would try to seal over the wound, whatever it was, and I would be lulled into sleep, surrounded by my toys, my Big Little Books, my stacks of drawings crayoned on the rough dun-colored paper supplied at school, and the Vernon Grant figures presiding above the bookshelf—a band of cheerful, long-nosed angels who lived in giant shoes and tumbled downhill. Paper, I felt, would protect me. Sometimes in my parents' room there were quarrels, stifled sobs from my melodious mother and percussive rumbling from my father; these troubles were like a thunderstorm that whipped and thumped the house for half an hour and then rolled off into the sky to the east, toward Philadelphia.

One center of trouble, I remember, was a man called Otto Werner, which Otto pronounced as if the "W" were a "V." Among the Pennsylvania Germans, he was exceptionally German, with a toothbrush mustache, a malicious twinkle in his eye, and an erect, jerky way of carrying himself. He, too, was a schoolteacher, but not in our town's system. He and my father, on weekends and in the summer, travelled to Philadelphia, an hour and a half away, to accumulate credits toward a master's degree. Having a master's would improve my father's salary by a few sorely needed dollars.

The first scandal that attached itself to Otto concerned his standing on the steps of the Van Pelt Library at the University of Pennsylvania and shouting, "*Heil, Hitler!*" The United States was not yet in the war, and a pro-German Band openly met in our local city of Alton, but still it was an eccentric and dangerous thing to do. Otto was, my father admitted, "a free spirit." However, he owned a car, and we did not. We once did—a green Model A that figures in my earliest memories—but somewhere in the Thirties it disappeared. In a town so compact one could walk anywhere within fifteen minutes, and in a region webbed with trolley tracks and train tracks, the deprivation did not seem radical. Once the war came, those who owned cars couldn't buy gas anyway.

A worse scandal than "*Heil, Hitler!*" had to do with a girl at the high school. My father carried a few notes from Otto to her, and it turned out they were love notes, and he was aiding and abetting the corruption of a minor. The girl's parents got involved, and members of the school board were informed. Not only could my father get fired, as I understood it: he could go to jail for his part in this scandal. As I lay in my bed at night I could hear my parents talking in a ragged, popping murmur like the noise of something frying; I could feel the heat, and my father twisting in his agony, and the other adults in the house holding their breath. Had there been trysts, and had my father carried the notes that arranged them? It was like him; he was always doing people unnecessary favors. Once he walked out into a snowstorm to go and apologize to a boy in one of his classes with whom he had been impatient, or sarcastic. "I hate sarcasm," he said. "Everybody in this part of the world uses it, but it hurts like hell to be on the receiving end. Poor kid, I thought he stunk the place up to get my goat, but upon sober reflection I believe it was just one more case of honest stupidity." His subject was chemistry, with its many opportunities for spillage, breakage, smells, and small explosions.

The scandal with the girl somehow died away. Perhaps the notes he carried were innocent. Perhaps he persuaded the principal and the school board that he, at least, was innocent. There had been a romance, because within a year or two the girl, graduated now, married Otto. The couple moved to the Southwest but occasionally would visit my parents. When my mother became a widow, living alone in a farmhouse ten miles from the town, the couple would visit her, as part of their annual Eastern pilgrimage. Though fifteen years younger, Mrs. Werner went plump early, and her hair turned white, so the age difference became less and less scandalous. They had bought a Winnebago and would pull up alongside the barn and Otto would limp across the yard to greet my mother merrily, that twinkle still in his eye. My mother would be merry in turn, having forgotten, it seemed, all the woe he once brought us. In trying to recall the heat in the old house, the terror he had caused, I have forgotten the most interesting thing about him: he had only one leg. The other was a beige prosthesis that gave him his jerky walk, a sharp hitch as if he were tossing something with his right hip. Remembering this makes him seem less dangerous: how could the world ever punish a one-legged man for shouting "*Heil,* Hitler!" or for falling in love with a teen-ager from another school system?

The country ran on dimes and quarters. A hamburger cost ten cents, and I paid ten cents to get into the movie house, until a war tax made it eleven. The last year of the war, a month before V-E Day and Hitler's vanishing—poof!—from his underground bunker, I turned thirteen, and old Mrs. Naftziger in the little glass booth somehow knew it. An adult ticket cost twenty-seven cents, and that was too much for me to go twice a week.

The economics of my grandfather's household seemed simple: my father brought home his pay every other week in a brown envelope, and the money was dumped in a little red-and-white recipe box that sat on top of the icebox. Anybody who needed money fished it out of the box; each lunchtime I was allowed six cents, a nickel and a penny, to buy a Tastykake on the way back to elementary school. My grandfather did the packaged-food shopping at Tyse Segner's store, a few houses away. Tyse, who lived in the back rooms and upstairs with his wife, was a man of my grandfather's generation—a rather ill-tempered one, I thought, considering all the candy he had behind his counter and could eat for free whenever he wanted. My mother, usually, bought fresh meat and vegetables at Bud Hoffert's Acme, two blocks away, past the ice plant, up on Second Street. Bud wore rimless glasses and a bloody apron. My grandmother did the cooking but never shopped; nor did my father—he just brought home, as he said, "the bacon." The little tin recipe box never became so empty that I had to do without my noontime Tastykake. I moved a kitchen chair next to the icebox to stand on while I fished the nickel and the penny from the box, beneath a clutter of folded dollars and scattered quarters. When the tin bottom began to show, more coins and bills somehow appeared, to tide us over, and these, it slowly dawned on me, were borrowed from the high-school sports receipts.

My father was in charge of them, as an extracurricular duty: at football games he would sit at a gap in the ropes, selling tickets and making change from a flat green box whose compartments were curved to let your fingers scoop up the coins. At basketball games he would sit with the box at a little table just inside the school's front portals, across from the glass case of silver trophies and around the corner from the supervising principal's office. The green box would come home with him, many nights, for safekeeping. The tickets fascinated me—great wheels of them, as wide as dinner plates but thicker. They came in two distinct colors, blue for adults and orange for students, and each ticket was numbered. It was another kind of money. Each rectangle of the thin, tightly coiled cardboard possessed, at the right time, a real value, brought into play by a sports event; money and time and cardboard and people's desire to *see* were magically interwoven. My father was magical, converting into dollars and quarters and dimes the Tuesday- and Friday-night basketball crowds and the outdoor crowd that straggled out of the town's streets onto the football field on Saturday afternoon. (It was easy to sneak under the ropes, but many grown-ups didn't bother, and paid.) The tickets, numbered in the hundreds, were worth nothing until he presided at his little table. He always made the balance right when he got his paycheck, or so he assured my mother. She had begun to get alarmed, and her alarm spread to me.

My memories of their conversations, the *pressure* of them, have me leaning my face against the grain of the wooden icebox, a zinc-lined cabinet whose dignity dominated our kitchen as it majestically digested, day after day, a succession of heavy ice blocks fetched in a straw-lined truck and carried with tongs into the house by a red-cheeked man with a leather apron down his back, to ward off the wet and the chill. I could feel the coldness on my cheek, through the zinc and oak, as my parents' faces revolved above me and their voices clung to my brain.

"Embezzlement," my mother said, a word I knew only from the radio. "What good will you be to any of us in jail?"

"I make it square, right to the penny. Square on the button, every other week, when I get my envelope."

"Suppose Danny Haas some week decides to deposit the receipts on a Friday instead of a Monday? He'd ask and you'd be short."

Danny Haas, I knew, taught senior-high math and headed up the school athletics program. A short man who smoked cigars and wore suits with broad stripes, he was one of the righteous at the town's core. My tall father and he sometimes clowned together, because of their height discrepancy, but it was clear to me who had the leverage, the connections, the power to bring down.

"He won't, Lucy," my father was saying. Whenever he used my mother's name, it was a sign that he wanted to end the conversation. "Danny's like all these Dutchmen, a slave to habit. Anyway, we're not talking Carnegie-Mellon bucks here, we're talking relative peanuts." How much, indeed? A ten-dollar bill, in those days, looked like a fortune to me; I never saw a twenty, not even when the recipe box was fullest.

"Nobody will think it's peanuts if it's missing."

My father became angry, as much as he ever did. "What can I do, Lucy? We live poor as dump dogs anyway." The phrase "dump dogs" had to be one he had brought from his other life, when he had lived in another state and been a boy like me. He went on, venting grievances seldom expressed in my hearing. "We've got a big place here to heat. We can't all go naked. The kid keeps growing. My brown suit is wearing out. Mom does what she can in her garden, but I've got five mouths to feed." He called my grandmother "Mom" and exempted her, I felt, from the status of pure burden. My mother's work at her wicker desk produced no money, my grandfather in his pride had bought too big a house, and I—I didn't even go out and shovel snow for neighbors in a storm, because I was so susceptible to colds. My father was warming to his subject. "Count 'em—five *Nihil ex nihilo,* Dad used to say." "Dad" was his own father, dead before I was born. "You don't get something for nothing," he translated. "There are no free rides in this life."

My mother feebly used the word "economize," another radio word, but even I could feel it was hopeless; how could I go without my Tastykake when nobody else in my class was that poor? My father had to go on stealing from the school, and would someday be chased in his barrel down the Town Hall steps.

During the war things eased a bit. Men were scarce, and he got summer jobs that did not aggravate his hernia; he was made a timekeeper for a railroad work crew. The tracks were humming and needed to be kept up. In the history books our time in the war seems short: less than four years from Pearl Harbor to V-J Day. Yet it seemed to go on forever, while I inched up through the grades of elementary school. It became impossible to imagine a world without the war, without the big headlines and the ration tokens and coupons and the tin-can drives and Bing Crosby and Dorothy Lamour selling War Bonds at rallies. I reached seventh grade, a junior-high grade, housed in the grand yellow brick building where my father taught.

I was too young for chemistry, but there was no missing his high head and long stride in the halls. Sharing the waxed, locker-lined halls with him all day, being on his work premises, as it were, did not eradicate my anxiety that he would be brought low. The perils surrounding him became realer to me. We students filled the halls with a ruthless, trampling sound. My father was not a good disciplinarian; he was not

Pennsylvania-German enough, and took too little pleasure in silence and order. Entire classes, rumor reached me from the upper grades, were wasted in monologues in which he tried to impart the lessons that life had taught him—you don't get something for nothing, there are no free rides. These truths were well-illustrated in the workings of chemistry, so perhaps he wasn't as far off the point as the students thought. They played a game, of "getting him going," and thus sparing themselves classwork for the day. He would suddenly throw a blackboard eraser up toward the ceiling and with a boyish deftness catch it, saying, "What goes up must come down." He told the momentarily silenced students, "You're on top of Fools' Hill now, but you'll come down the other side, I promise you." He did not conceal from them his interest in the fruitful possibilities of disorder; so many great chemical discoveries, after all, were accidents. He loved chemistry. "Water is the universal solvent," I often heard him pronounce, as if it were a truly consoling formula, like "This, too, will pass away." Who is to say his message did not cut through the classroom confusion— the notes being passed, the muttered asides of the class clown, the physical tussles at the rear of the room?

He was the faculty clown, to my discomfort. His remarks in assembly always got the students laughing, and, in the spring, in the annual faculty-assembly program, he participated in a, to me, horrifying performance of the Pyramus and Thisbe episode of *A Midsummer Night's Dream*. Gotten up as a gawky, dirndl-clad, lipsticked Thisbe, in a reddish-blond wig with pigtails, my father climbed a short stepladder to reach the chink in the Wall. The Wall was played by the thickset football coach, Tank Geiger, wearing a football helmet and a sheet painted to resemble masonry.

I had noticed in the privacy of our home how my father's legs, especially where his stockings rubbed, were virtually hairless compared with those of other men. Now the sight of his hairless legs, bare for all to see, as he mounted the ladder—the students around me howling at every mincing step he took upward—made me think his moment to topple had come.

Mr. Geiger held up at arm's height a circle-forming thumb and forefinger to represent the chink in the wall; on the opposite side of the wall, little Mr. Haas climbed his ladder a step higher than my father, to put his face on the same level. "O, kiss me," he recited, "through the hole of this vile wall." Mr. Geiger mugged in mock affront, and the auditorium rocked. My father, in his high Thisbe voice, answered, "I kiss the wall's hole, not your lips at all," and his and Mr. Haas's faces slowly met through the third teacher's fingers. The screams of disbelieving hilarity around me made my ears burn. I shut my eyes. This had to be ruinous, I thought. This was worse than any of my dreams.

But the next day my father loped through the halls with his head high, his hair parted in the middle as usual, in his usual shiny suit, and school life continued. "Burning," went another of his chemical slogans, "destroys nothing. It just shuffles the molecules."

When he was not in his classroom, I discovered, he was in the boiler room. There was a faculty room, with a long table, where the teachers could sit and rest in an idle class period; but they couldn't smoke there, and many of the male teachers took their time off in the boiler room, a great two-story chamber beneath the towering smokestack. A subterranean passage led into it from the school basement, past the woodworking shop, but as a mere student, a seventh-grader, I only entered, in search of my father, from the outside. You crossed a stretch of concrete enlivened by a few basketball backboards fastened flat onto the bricks, opened a resistant metal door, and stepped, with a hollow sound, onto the landing at the head of a flight of studded steel stairs. In front of you, across a dizzying gap, were the immense coal-burning furnaces that warmed the school. You could see the near furnace take a great sliding gulp of pea coal from its hopper, and the mica viewing-portals shudder with orange incandescence, and bundles of asbestos-wrapped steam pipes snake across the ceiling. Dwarfed by the downward perspective, a few male teachers sat and smoked around a card table, in company with the school janitors.

His coat off, and the full length of the parting in his hair visible, my father looked youthfully happy, sunk to the concrete bottom of this warm volume of space. The rising heat intensified my blush of shyness as I descended, breaching the male sanctuary with my message. Why I was intruding I have forgotten, but I remember receiving a genial welcome, as if I were already one of these men who had filled the glass ashtrays to overflowing and whose coffee cups had left a lace of brown circles on the card-table top. As a teacher's child I was privileged to peek behind the formal stage-set of education's daily theatre. It was a slight shock to see, on the stained table, a deck of worn pinochle cards, held together by a rubber band. Teachers were human. I was expected to become, eventually, one of them.

At the war's end, we moved from the house that was too big to a farmhouse, ten miles away, that was too small. It was my mother's idea of economizing. The antique small-town certainties I had grown up among were abruptly left behind. No more wood icebox, no more tin toaster, no more Vernon Grant nursery rhymes framed above my bed, no more simply running down through the yard to the high school. My father and I were thrown together in a state of daily exile, getting into the car—we had to acquire a car—before the frost had left the windshield and returning, many nights, after dusk, our headlights the only ones on the pitted dirt road home. He still took the ticket money at the basketball games, and, as another extracurricular duty, coached the swimming team, which, since the school had no pool, practiced at the YMCA in Alton's dingy and menacing downtown. The ten-year-old car we acquired kept giving us adventures: flat tires, broken axles, fearful struggles to put on tire chains at the base of a hill in the midst of a snowstorm. We sometimes didn't make it home, and walked and hitchhiked to shelter—the homes of other teachers, or what my father cheerfully called "fleabag" hotels. We became, during those years of joint commuting, a kind of team—partners in peril, fellow-sufferers on the edge of disaster. It was dreadful and yet authentic to be stuck in a stalled car with only four dollars between us, in the age before ATMs. It was—at least afterwards, in the hotel, where my father had successfully begged the clerk to call Danny Haas to vouch for us—bliss, a rub against basic verities, an instance of survival.

I stood in sardonic, exasperated silence during his conversations with hotel clerks, garage mechanics, diner waitresses, strangers on the street, none of whom were accustomed to encountering such a high level of trust. It was no mistake that he had wound up in education; he believed that everyone had something to teach him. His suppliant air humiliated me, but I was fourteen, fifteen; I was at his mercy, and he was at the mercy of the world. I saw him rebuffed and misunderstood. Flecks of foam would appear at the corners of his mouth as he strove to communicate; in my helpless witnessing I was half blinded by impatience and what now seems a fog of love, a pity bulging toward him like some embarrassing warpage of my own face.

He enjoyed human contact even at its least satisfactory, it slowly came to me. "I just wanted to see what he would come up with," he would explain after some futile tussle with, say, the policeman in charge of the municipal garage to which our non-starting car had been towed, parked as it had been in a loading zone by the railroad platform; the cop refused to grasp the distinction between my father's good intentions and the car's mechanical misbehavior. "I used to land in the damnedest little towns," he would tell me, of his days selling china. "In upstate New York, West Virginia, wherever, you'd just get off the train with your sample case and go into any store where you saw china and try to talk them into carrying your line, which usually cost a bit more than the lines they had. You never knew what would happen. Some of them, in these dumps at the back of nowhere, would come up with the most surprising orders—tall orders. This was before the Depression hit, of course. I mean, it hit in '29, but there was a grace period before it took hold. And then you were born. Young America. Your mother and I, it knocked us for a loop, we had never figured on ourselves as parents. I don't know why not—it happens all the time. Making babies is the number-one priority for human nature. When I'm standing up there trying to pound the periodic table into their jiggling heads I think to myself, 'These poor devils, they just want to be making babies!' "

My own developing baby-making yen took the form, first, of learning to smoke. You couldn't get anywhere, in the high-school society of the late Forties, without smoking. I had bought a pack—Old Golds, I think, because of the doubloons—at the Alton railroad station, while my father was coaching the swimming team. Though the first drags did, in his phrase, knock me for a loop, I stuck with it; my vagabond life as his satellite left me with a lot of idle time in luncheonette booths. One winter morning when I was fifteen, I asked him if I could light up a cigarette in the car on the way to school. He himself had stopped, on his doctor's advice. But he didn't say no to me, and, more than thirty years after I, too, quit, I still remember those caustic, giddying drags mixed with the first grateful whiffs of warmth from the car heater, while the little crackling radio played its medley of farm reports and Hit Parade tunes. His tacit permission, coming from a schoolteacher, would have been viewed, we both knew, as something of a disgrace. But it was my way of becoming a human being, and part of being human is being on the verge of disgrace.

Moving to the country had liberated us both, I see now, from the small-town grid and those masters of righteousness. The shopping fell to us, and my father favored a roadside grocery store that was owned and run, it was rumored, by a former Alton gangster. Like my father, Arty Callahan was tall, melancholy, and slightly deaf; his wife was an overweight, wisecracking woman whose own past, it was said, had been none too savory. My father loved them, and loved the minutes of delay their store gave him on the return to our isolated country home. Both Mr. and Mrs. Callahan took him in the right way, it seemed to me, with not too much of either amusement or gravity; they were, all three, free spirits. While he talked to them, acting out, in gestures and phrases that had become somewhat stylized, his sense of daily peril, I would sit at a small Formica-topped table next to the magazine rack and leaf through *Esquire,* looking for Vargas girls. I would sneak a look at Arty Callahan's profile, so noncommittally clamped over his terribly false teeth, and wonder how many men he had killed. The only gangsterish thing he did was give me ten dollars—a huge amount for an hour's work—for tutoring his son in algebra on Saturdays, when I was old enough to drive the car there.

We had traded in our car for a slightly newer and more dependable one, though still a pre-war model. By the time I went off to college I no longer feared—I no longer dreamed—that my father would be savaged by society. He was fifty by then, a respectable age. Living his life beside him for five years, I had seen that his flirtation with disgrace was only that, not a ruinous infatuation. Nothing but death could topple him, and even that not very far, not in my mind.

As long as I have been in the White House, I can't help waking at 5 a.m. and hearing the old man at the foot of the stairs calling and telling me to get out and milk the cows.

—HARRY S. TRUMAN

Only A Dad

Only a dad, with a tired face,
Coming home from the daily race,
Bringing little of gold or fame,
To show how well he has played the game,
But glad in his heart that his own rejoice
To see him come, and to hear his voice.

Only a dad, with a brood of four,
One of ten million men or more.
Plodding along in the daily strife,
Bearing the whips and the scorns of life,
With never a whimper of pain or hate,
For the sake of those who at home await.

Only a dad, neither rich nor proud,
Merely one of the surging crowd
Toiling, striving from day to day,
Facing whatever may come his way,
Silent, whenever the harsh condemn,
And bearing it all for the love of them.

Only a dad, but he gives his all
To smooth the way for his children small,
Doing, with courage stern and grim,
The deeds that his father did for him.
This is the line that for him I pen,
Only a dad, *but the best of men.*

—EDGAR A. GUEST

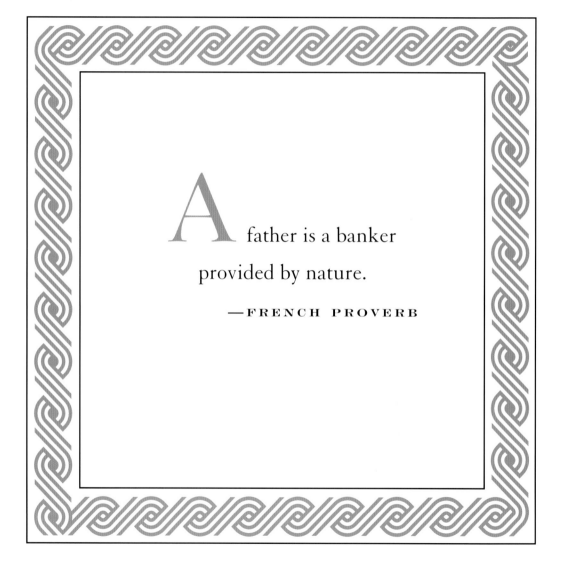

A father is a banker
provided by nature.

—FRENCH PROVERB

Robert Louis Stevenson (age 16)

1866

RESPECTED PATERNAL RELATIVE,

I write to make a request of the most moderate nature. Every year I have cost you an enormous—nay, elephantine—sum of money for drugs and physician's fees, and the most expensive time of the twelve months was March.

But this year the biting Oriental blasts, the howling tempests, and the general ailments of the human race have been successfully braved by yours truly.

Does not this deserve remuneration?

I appeal to your charity, I appeal to your generosity, I appeal to your justice, I appeal to your accounts, I appeal, in fine, to your purse.

My sense of generosity forbids the receipt of more—my sense of justice forbids the receipt of less—than half-a-crown. Greeting from, Sir, your most affectionate and needy son, R. STEVENSON

Memories of
My Father

BY HENRY DICKENS

N THE YEAR 1869, after I had been at college about a year, I was fortunate enough to gain one of the principal scholarships at Trinity Hall, Cambridge—not a great thing, only £50 a year; but I knew that this success, slight as it was, would give him intense pleasure, so I went to meet him at Higham Station upon his arrival from London to tell him of it. As he got out of the train I told him the news. He said, 'Capital! capital!'—nothing more. Disappointed to find that he received the news apparently so lightly, I took my seat beside him in the pony carriage he was driving. Nothing more happened until we had got half-way to Gad's Hill, when he broke down completely. Turning towards me with tears in his eyes and giving me a warm grip of the hand, he said, 'God bless you, my boy; God bless you!' That pressure of the hand I can feel now as distinctly as I felt it then, and it will remain as strong and real until the day of my death.

To My Father:
What I've Never Said

BY JOYCE CAROL OATES

It must have been when I was in my early thirties
that I first realized this simple and profound truth—
You should be me.

The thought swept over me leaving me faint!
I don't mean *I should be you,* still less
I should have been you.
Only just *You should be me.* The writer, the
        teacher. The one who has made a life,
        & how cherished a life, of literature.

It didn't happen that way.
You were born in 1914, I was born in 1938.
You were born poor & had to quit school when you were a boy.

The Depression hit your generation & you.
Assembly-line worker. Tool & dye designer.
Professional sign painter.
Orchard-keeper.
& through the decades, a reader of passion and zest.
The reader for whom every writer writes.
& after your retirement, for 15 years you were a student
                auditing courses at the State University at Buffalo
& you were the student for whom every teacher yearns.
You loved books & you loved your professors.
Now you no longer take the bus to the University,
& you no longer read ambitious books.
"Macular degeneration."
But can it be cured?
Please tell me it can be cured!
Though you still read, slowly. At your ingenious magnifying
                machine. The book's page suffused with light & the
                type enlarged.

I see your face in mine, Daddy. I hear your yearning in my own.
Your love of the imagination, your wild & unpredictable
                    sense of humor.
Your stubbornness, your inviolable pride & integrity.
Your unexpected eloquence—"I take 17 pills through a single
                    day. I'm held together by pharmaceutal glue."
Your droll dark humor now, in your mid-80s, & I
                    just turned unimaginable 60, we talk together
                              frankly
                    as we'd never talked before.
As if, with time, we grow closer in age to each other.
As if, with time, the old distinctions between us melt away.

"These nights, I can't read prose very well. I guess I won't
get through your new novel. It's wonderful and I love it but
my eyes . . . I read poetry. In the college anthologies.
Frost, Dickinson, Whitman. Sandburg. That's how I spend
my nights, now."

A Memory of
Two Fathers

—·•◁∞▷•·—

BY SHAUN O'CONNELL

I WAITED next to a huge boulder at the hollow of two hills, watching the two men who stood, tall and imposing, on the sixth tee. The late-afternoon sun burned behind them as they contemplated their tee shots on this down-and-up-hill par-five and they cast long shadows towards me. I squinted and concentrated, as I knew a good caddie should, so I would be able to follow the flight of their shots, which should land in the fairway, to my left, beyond the boulder. On the boulder was painted MCC in huge letters, for Marlborough Country Club, and the fairway was burned brown, for this was August.

It was 1946, the summer after the war. I was eleven. Vin, my father, then in his early forties, a wandering man, was back from four years of wartime service as a Navy sailor in the Seabees. Cliff, my uncle, then in his mid-fifties, a dependable man, had been too old for wartime service, so he stayed at his job, working for the United Shoe Machinery Company. Vin built landing strips under Japanese fire on South Pacific islands, while Cliff oversaw the repairs of shoe machinery in shops scattered throughout towns in central Massachusetts.

Vin was a dreamy, boozy Celt, seldom there when you needed him, but often charming. When he wasn't squeezed by the vice of depression, Vin laughed frequently and cried occasionally, but mainly he talked his way through life, telling wonderful stories—many of them true. Cliff was a practical, abstemious, New England Yankee, always there for you, but not much fun. Though Cliff was frugal with words and emotions, he was a man who meant what he said. Cliff gave an honest day's work for his day's pay and he never questioned the right of an employer to set the wage rate, but Vin jumped from job to job, avoided heavy lifting and complained about exploitation. Vin was prodigal, unreliable, and winning: "Let a smile be your umbrella," he told me, "and you'll have a wet face." Cliff, suspicious of joy, was circumspect and austere: "there's a right way and a wrong way to do everything," he told me repeatedly. Cliff was morning, a glaring sun, and Vin was night, a blue moon. Their alternating presences filled my sky. Now they stood together, upon a hill, in late-summer twilight, playing the same game, while I carried their golf bags.

After my mother died when I was a baby, Vin had entrusted the care of his only son to his older sister, Jane, and her husband, Cliff. So, as I thought of it, I had two "fathers" to show me the way. But which way? Now, at long last, I might find out, for we were all together, just as I had so often dreamed during the war. The lights had gone on again, all over the world, just as Vaughn Monroe, with his foggy voice, sang in the song that ran through my mind as I watched Vin take his long, graceful, Bobby Jones-style swing, which he had learned from a Florida golf pro in the 1920s. "That's *it,*" I thought, as his clubhead silently came down upon the ball.

Vin's hair had gone gray and he now carried more weight, but his smooth swing still ended in a classic, hands-high body turn. At the same time I heard the belated *crack* of his hit, I was amazed to see his drive soar high over the boulder, dead on line with the distant pin; then his ball hit on the up-slope of the fairway and bounced into a trap, some 250 yards from the tee. Though I had been caddying all that summer, I had never seen a drive so long, so risky, so doomed—for the trap was gouged into the hill like a bomb crater. When his ball stopped, half-embedded in sand, I looked back, up the hill to the tee, and saw Vin, annoyed, toss away his driver, then turn his back, cup his hands and light a Lucky, as though that—a great drive, hit long, low and straight at the hole, but ending up stuck, deep in a trap—was about all he might expect from a life of bad fortune. Vin wasn't even watching when Cliff hit, though I was.

Cliff had a different style of swing. Stiffened by years of deskwork and commuting, Cliff had learned the game on his own, in his fifties, so he developed a short stab at the ball, a jerky whip which looked like the swing a right-handed batter uses when he chokes up on his bat and punches a hit to right field. Cliff's drives were chopped out 150 yards, while Vin's drives soared and, like Ted Williams' home runs, hung suspended, then dropped at impossible distances. I didn't have to worry about spotting Cliff's golf balls, which always fell near mid-fairway, but Vin's shots could come down anywhere—left or right side rough, woods, water. Or, rarely, they reached long and straight, far past Cliff's humpy shots.

Sure enough, Cliff's shot, accompanied by a grunt, as though he were pushing open a stuck door, dropped into the fairway—safe, sure and short. Two more like it and he would have a chip and a putt for a possible par. But Vin's score could be anything from an eagle to a triple bogey.

Vin, born in 1903, was the petted, youngest son in a family of six children; his father, an Irish immigrant from Cork, worked for the railroad. Before Vin left home, his sainted mother sprinkled him with holy water, to protect him on his journeys. She must have sensed how difficult his voyages would become.

Cliff, born in 1890, was the steady, eldest son in a family of three children; his father was a solid Yankee farmer. A lapsed Episcopalian, Cliff needed no holy water for his journeys. He never left the home in which he was born; nor did he stray from the straight and narrow path he set for himself. At age thirteen Cliff quit school to labor in a shoe factory; then he became a whiz at machine repair and so he made that his life's work. Cliff, in his only rash act, crossed the region's ethnic line to marry a pretty Irish American, a young woman from nearby Framingham, Jane O'Connell. By doing so, Cliff allowed into his life an astonishing range of Celtic intemperance, wit and eruptions of powerful feelings.

Cliff hunched over, wagged his three-wood, and whacked his ball up the fairway, not far above the trap in which Vin's shot had landed. Vin walked up to the deep trap and studied his shot, shaking his head in dismay. A huge lip of grass hung over the top of the trap and a clump of trees stood, ominously, between his ball and the green.

"You gonna chip it out to the side of the trap?" I asked.

"That what you think I should do?"

"Well, uh, yuh, I guess," I said, with my characteristic conviction and eloquence.

He tossed away his inevitable Lucky, flashed his wry smile and said, "That's not what I'm going to do, Sonny Boy. Stand back and keep your eye on the ball."

He took a seven-iron, a club which would give his ball both loft and distance; then he set himself and swung, down and through, blasting the sand. Wondrously, his ball cleared the lip of the trap and lifted off in flight toward the green, but I winced when, just before flying free of the trees, it clipped a branch of an elm and caromed off to the side, onto the fairway, seventy-five yards behind Cliff's second shot.

"Almost cleared the trees," I said.

" 'Almost' doesn't count for much, does it?"

I didn't know, so I walked over to Vin's ball and waited for him to pick a club for his third shot.

During the 1920s, Vin worked as a chauffeur for the family of a Framingham railroad owner; Vin drove them in their Packard to Florida, where they wintered. To them he was more than an employee, but he was less than the adopted son he imagined himself; he learned the manners and tastes of those of the manor to which he was not born while he romanced one of the Irish maids. With his slicked-back, Valentino-style hair and his dapper duds, Vin made himself into a small-time Gatsby, for Vin too had a "heightened sensitivity to the promises of life." In a yellowing picture—which I have propped before me as I write—Vin still poses on a Florida golf course, beneath a palm tree, decked out in a dazzling white shirt and slacks, leaning on a putter, one ankle jauntily crossing the other, free hand on hip, flashing a no-flies-on-me smile.

Then, in his most reckless act, Vin gave up all that borrowed glamour. Like Cliff, Vin too married a pretty, young woman from Framingham. Vin took a job that required no travel and he made a home for their new baby—me. For a while Vin was happy, but soon his life fell apart.

When I was little more than a year old, in 1936, my mother had a miscarriage; infection set in and she died. So I lost a mother, a sibling and a home, but my father lost more. Never again would his world make sense. Grieving, drinking and restless, he was in no shape to care for me, then or later. After I was passed around among relatives, I finally stuck at my Aunt Jane's, in Marlborough. She and Cliff had tried but failed to have children, so, though they were then in their mid-forties, they welcomed me. There I stayed, throughout my school years, rooted in one perpetual place.

Late in the 1930s, by then a confirmed wanderer, Vin worked in Northern Ireland, on construction projects. On his way home, a German sub torpedoed his boat, so he became a fierce patriot. After Pearl Harbor, Vin was the first man from Framingham to enlist in the Navy, though at age thirty-eight he could have avoided the draft. Indeed, he managed to join up only by volunteering for the Seabees. Nothing would keep him home. Vin was always seeking a new life, beyond the blue horizon. Though he never forgot me. His censored mail arrived regularly during the war. No force, however, could tear Cliff away from his primary responsibilities: his home, his family and his work. Cliff was always *there,* a steady beacon, but Vin came and went, a sweeping arc of light.

Vin pulled a two-wood out of the golf bag, again flicked his Lucky into the grass, set himself, unwound his lovely swing and sent a shot buzzing, long and low, over the fairway rise. We all watched it hit, jump and roll onto the front edge of the green. I felt my heart lift and my eyes blur, for I had never before been so close to anything so marvelous as that shot, still vivid after all these years. Then Vin casually tossed me his club, as though he did this every day, and lit a fresh Lucky. Cliff, unspectacularly but predictably, jerked a three-wood shot into the air and watched it plop down, fifty yards short of the green.

Vin winked at me and yelled across to Cliff, lifting an imaginary glass. "I'll drink to that!" But Cliff looked down, looking for a divot to replace, pretending he did not hear.

Vin drank—crazily, self-destructively, seeking perfect oblivion—but Cliff was as sober and as just as a judge. Vin went off on bats—on wild, shore-leave drunks—and woke up in surprising places, finding himself without money, shaking and guilty, but briefly purged. (What a *dramatic* life Vin had, shot full of passionate intensities.) After he had been missing for days, he would turn up, reeling, while his sister cringed at the sight of him. Or she would get a call from one of his buddies, a solicitous bartender or even the police. She would then drive to Boston or Providence or Worcester, wherever Vin ended up, and bring him back to Marlborough to sleep it off. She would be furious at her wayward, younger brother, but Cliff would say nothing. (What a *quiet* life Cliff had, apart from all those Mick, in-law dramatics.)

When Vin came to, groggily, on his many mornings-after, he would make his way to the kitchen, where he boiled coffee, scrambled piles of eggs, fried stacks of bacon, toasted bread and ate it all with a focused passion. Then he would lean back from the kitchen table and silently smoke his Luckys—he held his cigarettes tip-down, so the smoke curled up through his fingers, leaving them sickly yellow. Eventually he would talk, at first to me, dutifully checking up on how I was doing in school, but edgy with this attentive lad whose presence reminded him of too many painful things; then, more familiarly. Vin would toss words, like flowers, at his sister's back as she moved about the kitchen, tense with disapproval. Vin would recall old times, before

World War I, when he and Jane were children—when the O'Connell kids played together in the horse barn or when she was supposed to keep him from giggling in church but often joined him. Soon my Aunt Jane, enticed from her sulk, would also settle down at the kitchen table—drinking coffee, smoking and "batting the breeze," as she called it, with her incorrigible but beloved brother. Cliff, of course, was off putting in another honest day's work, but I was there in the kitchen, with Jiggs, my dog, both of us alert, watching the pieces of my scattered world come together.

Sometimes Vin took me to Boston, on the Boston & Worcester bus, to a Red Sox game—Cliff preferred the less flashy Boston Braves—or to movies along Washington Street. (During ball games Vin spent many innings lining up to buy beers; during movies he would slip out for nips at nearby pubs.) Then, just like that, Vin's shore leave would be over. I would ride into Boston, sitting in the back of the Plymouth sedan with Jiggs, while Aunt Jane drove and Vin gabbed; at crowded South Station, he would wave and then disappear into a crowd of sailors and soldiers, off again to the war.

When Vin returned, he was often unable to make it past one of several barrooms—particularly the West End Café, at the bottom of the hill on which Cliff's house stood. When he did make it home, sometimes Vin woke me in the middle of the night, gripped me, breathed boozy fumes, cried and told me *never, never* to forget my mother—a woman I could not remember. On other days, when I got up to let Jiggs out, I would find Vin asleep on our lawn, under a pear tree, unable or unwilling to enter Cliff's house. His sister would blush with shame at what the neighbors might think.

Cliff took a drink only once in my presence. One blistering, August day, when I was nine or ten and he was on his two-week vacation, he was uncharacteristically idle, between home improvements projects—how I used to dread the labors of his vacations—and sweltering in the summer heat. "I want a glass of beer," he declared.

I was amazed. Surrounded by Irish blatherers and drinkers, Cliff was a strong, silent man who distrusted the lifts of language or liquor.

"Well, are you going to stand there with your mouth open, catching flies, or are you coming with me?"

I closed my mouth and went with him. Cliff set his summer straw hat on his head. He bought a new hat every summer; he donned it every Memorial Day and, every Labor Day, he punched a hole in the hat and threw it away; he wore it straight and flat, the way Buster Keaton wore his porkpie hat, and Cliff had Keaton's deadpan, though no one ever laughed at my uncle and got away with it. That's the kind of man he was.

The West End Café was full of louts and layabouts, card players and bull throwers, the usual crowd—many of them Vin's drinking buddies. "So how's your old man?" one barfly asked me, until he was silenced by my uncle's glare. Cliff ordered his dime beer and a nickel Coke for me. I stood by, breathing in the acid odor of cigarettes and the stink of beer, trying to figure all this out. Cliff drank down his beer as if it were a glass of lemonade. Then he ordered another and drank *half* a glass. He then smoked a Camel, holding it between his lips, straight out, never inhaling, talking to no one. After his one and a half beers and his cigarette, he did a stunning thing: he tipped his straw hat back an inch, revealing a red line across his brow—a shocking violation of his self-imposed dress code.

"Are you going to drink that or hold it all afternoon?" he asked me.

"I'm not thirsty," I said.

"Then don't drink it," he said.

So that was it. Cliff only drank beer because he was *thirsty* on this hot summer day. After a beer and a half, his thirst was slaked and he was ready to leave. Why else would a man stay? We trudged back up the hill to our home, to take up a man's proper tasks (wallpapering, roof-tarring, drainage-ditch digging, floor-sanding). I wondered why Vin, my "real" father, drank so much. Maybe he was gripped by a thirst so fierce that no amount of booze could drown it, a thirst so deep that Cliff could never understand. Cliff had brought me to that tavern, Vin's tavern, to show me just how much beer an honorable man needs. But I knew from Vin's example that there was more mystery to it than that. Between the lessons of my two fathers, I was simultaneously intrigued and repelled by alcohol.

On a Christmas Eve, late in World War II, Vin, home on leave, grew restless. I was picking my way through a piano performance of "White Christmas" while the elders in my odd family sat in attendance. We were all in the "front room," where all of my aunt's "nice things" and the decorated Christmas tree were on display. Impatient, annoyed at hearing again that moving tune, which Tokyo Rose had played repeatedly to American troops who listened to her from the Solomon Islands, Vin began idly to examine his sister's knickknacks that cluttered every table. He was, by then, drunk, awash in his own private griefs. He discovered a figurine of a cat with Made in Japan painted on the bottom, brooded over it and then hurled it against a wall. Then he lurched around the room, cursing and searching for more ceramics to shatter, while I hurriedly concluded my concert. "May all your Christmases be bright!" Soon all the offending knickknacks were smashed, and so was Vin, who was helped off to bed by his furious sister. Cliff, a cigarette clenched in his lips, watched all this, never saying a word, but I could see the ire in his narrowed eyes as Vin staggered past.

So I was not surprised, that afternoon after the war on the golf course, when Cliff was again silent after Vin joked about drinking.

Cliff was off the green in three shots and Vin was on the green, two putts away from a par. I did not know which man to root for. I couldn't help but be impressed by Vin's grace, dash and willingness to take risks, but I knew he was here today and gone tomorrow. I knew too that Cliff's slow and steady ways made my world safe, if a bit dull. Indeed, I never have been sure which way to go, so I have been, at various times, each of my fathers—cautious here, rash there, pulled this way and that by the voices and images of these men in my head.

That day they played out that hole in silence. Cliff took a long time with his fourth shot—clearly it mattered. His chip, gently scooped rather than poked, was an occasion of rare beauty in the life of a man who set more value in efficiency than grace. It hit and held, two feet from the cup. Vin, clearly impressed, nodded respectfully at Cliff, then took his putter from me and, without hesitation, knocked his putt toward the cup. Its speed and distance were perfect. The ball curved up over a rise and dropped slowly, right on line—but, at the last moment, it rimmed the cup and stayed out, hanging on the edge. Vin smiled sardonically—of course!—and tapped in his ball. Then Cliff took his putter from me. For some reason, my stomach ached. Again pausing, always considering, Cliff deliberately rolled in his two-foot putt. I felt a sudden release. Each of my fathers, each in his own characteristic way, had parred the hole. There was, after all, as my Aunt Jane liked to say, more than one way to skin a cat.

Vin never made it to age fifty. He died in the spring of 1950, in his forty-seventh year, of carbon monoxide poisoning, in his father's house. The Certificate of Death said it was "accidental," but I know it was not. The doors to the kitchen, where Vin died, were closed. I know he had had enough disappointments and losses—he had raved enough, smashed enough and finally had enough to drink—so he slipped away while no one was watching. No farewell note, just a half-empty bottle of rye on the table to be remembered by. I was angry at him then, but I am getting over it.

Six years later, Cliff died of lung cancer, at age sixty-six. Though he did not inhale, all those cigarettes clenched between his lips leaked enough poison into his lungs to do him in. During his last months, I drove Cliff into Boston for radiation treatments at Massachusetts General Hospital and saw the startling deterioration of this once tall and stiff man into a bent, withered being, a man who needed to be helped to walk. However, during his final hours my impressive uncle rose from his death bed and, in withering pain, led me down to the basement of his house to show me where the water level had to be set to keep the oil burner from exploding. Cliff was determined to show me the right way to take care of things when he was gone.

Neither Vin, for all his blarney, nor Cliff, for all his honesty, spoke with me about important things, but their lives sent cryptic messages which I am still trying to decode, more than three decades later. Each man has shaped my days and ways. Like Vin, I left my hometown in search of something. But, like Cliff, I never went far. The "important places" for me have been local. From Boston's western suburbs, I too have accompanied my children on trips to Boston to see the Red Sox—the Braves, surprisingly, skipped town—or the movies. However, I made sure that I stayed with my children for the full nine innings or the whole movies. Which is not to say that I am not my fathers' son. For years I drank like Vin, but then I took up sobriety, like Cliff. For years I smoked but, in memory of both my fathers, I finally quit. As Hamlet's father pursued him, so do the ghosts of these men haunt my imagination, like the faint, sweet odors of whiskey and cigarettes. I will not look on their likes again.

At age fifty-six I have now outlived Vin by ten years; when Cliff died, he was a decade older than I am now. So I hang suspended between my two fathers, between two different styles of swinging at the world—between rashness and rigidity, elegance and caution, excess and understatement—indeed, between two different kinds of love. Now, with both Cliff and Vin long gone, I seek the proper words to bring them back so that they might be with me again, as they were more than forty years ago, when I walked between them on the long fairways of Marlborough Country Club. I need both fathers beside me as I play the back nine. As they showed me, I try to keep my eye on the ball and my swing smooth. I try to know what does and does not count in the final score.

Fatherhood, like marriage, is a constant struggle against your limitations and self-interests. But the urge to be a perfect father is there, because your child is a perfect gift.

—KENT NERBURN

Vietnam's Postwar Legacy

BY KAREN SPEARS ZACHARIAS

ADDY WAS KILLED by mortar fire in Vietnam's Ia Drang Valley, July 24, 1966. The Army sent him home, via air mail, in a silver casket.

As a young girl, I grew up envisioning my father's brutal death. I imagined his cries. The smell of smoke. His blood seeping from his wounds to the dirt beneath his cot. Picturing the dense jungle overgrowth, I railed about how difficult it was for guardian angels to find him in such a god-forsaken place.

And I grew up resenting Vietnam and its people.

So it was with misgivings that I decided to go to my father's battlefield. I feared everything—the water, the people, their government, my own grief.

As the plane dropped within sight of the Mekong Delta, I elbowed my way to a window, half-expecting to see Viet Cong, wielding guns, shouting unintelligibly at me. Instead, I saw a quilted agriculture landscape, similar to farmland I'd viewed from American skies. But this was not America. This was Vietnam. The place where my father drew his last breath.

Later, as military officials ordered our group, Sons and Daughters in Touch, to form a straight line at customs, one of the widows traveling with us pulled on her bags and said: "I feel like I've come home."

I didn't understand her remark until days later when I stepped off a plane in the Central Highlands.

Just outside the remote village of Plei Me, I stood at the edge of a manioc field and looked out over the Ia Drang Valley, the place where Daddy's life had seeped away. The jungle stretched as far as the eye could see. Imagining the violence of war in such a beautiful place was hard. But there were remnants of it. Pieces of mortar. Rusted hinges from ammo boxes. Shards of shell casings.

I stood still as a gate post as wind whispered to the bushes. I remembered how Daddy smelled of Old Spice and sun-dried t-shirts. I recalled his laughter, how it made a room rumble. I felt as though my father was there, in that field, expecting me. Like I'd finally come home to him.

The pain of war does not cease when the bombing ends. I don't miss my father less with each passing year. I am simply more cognizant of all the life he's missed.

But never again will I envision Vietnam as a god-forsaken place. I won't dwell on it's blood-soaked soil or Daddy's cries as he lay dying.

Instead I will remember the sound of wind rushing through the dry grasses and the halting strains of "Yesterday," that lonesome Beatles tune, echoing through a village hut. I'll recall the sweet laughter of a boy as he herded a water buffalo down a red dirt road.

And I'll remember that my father died in a beautiful land fighting for the freedoms of a loving people.

My love for my father has never
been touched or approached by any other
love. I hold him in my heart of hearts as a
man apart from all other men, as one
apart from all other beings.

—MAMIE DICKENS, ABOUT HER
FATHER, CHARLES DICKENS

Little Women

BY LOUISA MAY ALCOTT

NOW AND THEN, in this work-a-day world, things do happen in the delightful story-book fashion, and what a comfort that is. Half an hour after every one had said they were so happy they could only hold one drop more, the drop came. Laurie opened the parlor door, and popped his head in very quietly. He might just as well have turned a somersault, and uttered an Indian war-whoop; for his face was so full of suppressed excitement, and his voice so treacherously joyful, that every one jumped up, though he only said, in a queer, breathless voice, "Here's another Christmas present for the March family."

Before the words were well out of his mouth, he was whisked away somehow, and in his place appeared a tall man, muffled up to the eyes, leaning on the arm of another tall man, who tried to say something and couldn't. Of course there was a general stampede; and for several minutes everybody seemed to lose their wits, for the strangest things were done, and no one said a word. Mr. March became invisible in the embrace of four pairs of loving arms; Jo disgraced herself by nearly fainting away, and had to be doctored by Laurie in the china closet; Mr. Brooke kissed Meg entirely by mistake, as he somewhat incoherently explained; and Amy, the dignified, tumbled over a stool, and, never stopping to get up, hugged and cried over her father's boots in the most touching manner. Mrs. March was the first to recover herself, and held up her hand with a warning, "Hush! remember Beth!"

But it was too late; the study door flew open,—the little red wrapper appeared on the threshold,—joy put strength into the feeble limbs,—and Beth ran straight into her father's arms. Never mind what happened just after that; for the full hearts overflowed, washing away the bitterness of the past, and leaving only the sweetness of the present.

It was not at all romantic, but a hearty laugh set everybody straight again,—for Hannah was discovered behind the door, sobbing over the fat turkey, which she had forgotten to put down when she rushed up from the kitchen. As the laugh subsided, Mrs. March began to thank Mr. Brooke for his faithful care of her husband, at which Mr. Brooke suddenly remembered that Mr. March needed rest, and, seizing Laurie, he precipitately retired. Then the two invalids were ordered to repose, which they did, by both sitting in one big chair, and talking hard.

Mr. March told how he had longed to surprise them, and how, when the fine weather came, he had been allowed by his doctor to take advantage of it; how devoted Brooke had been, and how he was altogether a most estimable and upright young man. Why Mr. March paused a minute just there, and, after a glance at Meg, who was violently poking the fire, looked at his wife with an inquiring lift of the eyebrows, I leave you to imagine; also why Mrs. March gently nodded her head, and asked, rather abruptly, if he wouldn't have something to eat. Jo saw and understood the look; and she stalked grimly away, to get wine and beef tea, muttering to herself, as she slammed the door, "I hate estimable young men with brown eyes!"

There never *was* such a Christmas dinner as they had that day. The fat turkey was a sight to behold, when Hannah sent him up, stuffed, browned and decorated. So was the plum-pudding, which quite melted in one's mouth; likewise the jellies, in which Amy revelled like a fly in a honey-pot. Everything turned out well; which was a mercy, Hannah said, "For my mind was that flustered, mum, that it's a mer-rycle I didn't roast the pudding and stuff the turkey with raisens, let alone bilin' of it in a cloth."

Mr. Laurence and his grandson dined with them; also Mr. Brooke,—at whom Jo glowered darkly, to Laurie's infinite amusement. Two easy-chairs stood side by side at the head of the table, in which sat Beth and her father, feasting, modestly, on chicken and a little fruit. They drank healths, told stories, sung songs, "reminisced," as the old folks say, and had a thoroughly good time. A sleigh-ride had been planned, but the girls would not leave their father; so the guests departed early, and, as twilight gathered, the happy family sat together round the fire.

"Just a year ago we were groaning over the dismal Christmas we expected to have. Do you remember?" asked Jo, breaking a short pause, which had followed a long conversation about many things.

"Rather a pleasant year on the whole!" said Meg, smiling at the fire, and congratulating herself on having treated Mr. Brooke with dignity.

"I think it's been a pretty hard one," observed Amy, watching the light shine on her ring, with thoughtful eyes.

"I'm glad it's over, because we've got you back," whispered Beth, who sat on her father's knee.

"Rather a rough road for you to travel, my little pilgrims, especially the latter part of it. But you have got on bravely; and I think the burdens are in a fair way to tumble off very soon," said Mr. March, looking, with fatherly satisfaction, at the four young faces gathered round him.

"How do you know? Did mother tell you?" asked Jo.

"Not much; straws show which way the wind blows; and I've made several discoveries today."

"Oh, tell us what they are!" cried Meg, who sat beside him.

"Here is one!" and, taking up the hand which lay on the arm of his chair, he pointed to the roughened forefinger, a burn on the back, and two or three little hard spots on the palm. "I remember a time when this hand was white and smooth, and your first care was to keep it so. It was very pretty then, but to me it is much prettier now,—for in these seeming blemishes I read a little history. A burnt offering has been made of vanity; this hardened palm has earned something better than blisters, and I'm sure the sewing done by these pricked fingers will last a long time, so much good-will went into the stitches. Meg, my dear, I value the womanly skill which keeps home happy, more than white hands or fashionable accomplishments; I'm proud to shake this good, industrious little hand, and hope I shall not soon be asked to give it away."

If Meg had wanted a reward for hours of patient labor, she received it in the hearty pressure of her father's hand, and the approving smile he gave her.

"What about Jo? Please say something nice; for she has tried so hard, and been so very, very good to me," said Beth, in her father's ear.

He laughed, and looked across at the tall girl who sat opposite, with an unusually mild expression in her brown face.

"In spite of the curly crop, I don't see the 'son Jo' whom I left a year ago," said Mr. March. "I see a young lady who pins her collar straight, laces her boots neatly, and neither whistles, talks slang, nor lies on the rug, as she used to do. Her face is rather thin and pale, just now, with watching and anxiety; but I like to look at it, for it has grown gentler, and her voice is lower; she doesn't bounce, but moves quietly, and takes care of a certain little person in a motherly way, which delights me. I rather miss my wild girl; but if I get a strong, helpful, tender-hearted woman in her place, I shall feel quite satisfied. I don't know whether the shearing sobered our black sheep, but I do know that in all Washington I couldn't find anything beautiful enough to be bought with the five-and-twenty dollars which my good girl sent me."

Jo's keen eyes were rather dim for a minute, and her thin face grew rosy in the firelight, as she received her father's praise, feeling that she did deserve a portion of it.

"Now Beth;" said Amy, longing for her turn, but ready to wait.

"There's so little of her I'm afraid to say much, for fear she will slip away altogether, though she is not so shy as she used to be," began their father, cheerfully; but, recollecting how nearly he *had* lost her, he held her close, saying, tenderly, with her cheek against his own, "I've got you safe, my Beth, and I'll keep you so, please God."

After a minute's silence, he looked down at Amy, who sat on the cricket at his feet, and said, with a caress of the shining hair,—

"I observed that Amy took drumsticks at dinner, ran errands for her mother all the afternoon, gave Meg her place to-night, and has waited on every one with patience and good-humor. I also observe that she does not fret much, nor prink at the glass, and has not even mentioned a very pretty ring which she wears; so I conclude that she has learned to think of other people more, and of herself less, and has decided to try and mould her character as carefully as she moulds her little clay figures. I am glad of this; for though I should be very proud of a graceful statue made by her, I shall be infinitely prouder of a lovable daughter, with a talent for making life beautiful to herself and others."

"What are you thinking of, Beth?" asked Jo, when Amy had thanked her father, and told about her ring.

"I read in 'Pilgrim's Progress' today, how, after many troubles, Christian and Hopeful came to a pleasant green meadow, where lilies bloomed all the year round, and there they rested happily, as we do now, before they went on to their journey's end," answered Beth: adding, as she slipped out of her father's arms, and went slowly to the instrument. "It's singing time now, and I want to be in my old place. I'll try to sing the song of the shepherd boy which the Pilgrims heard. I made the music for father, because he likes the verses."

So, sitting at the dear little piano, Beth softly touched the keys, and, in the sweet voice they had never thought to hear again, sung, to her own accompaniment, the quaint hymn, which was a singularly fitting song for her:—

"He that is down need fear no fall;
   He that is low no pride;
He that is humble ever shall
   Have God to be his guide.

"I am content with what I have,
   Little be it or much;
And, Lord! contentment still I crave,
   Because Thou savest such.

"Fulness to them a burden is,
   That go on Pilgrimage;
Here little, and hereafter bliss,
   Is best from age to age!

THE LAST TIME my dad and I were together I was in Nashville, where he and Mom lived. The two of us were in the car. He was driving, in his cowboy hat and coat. We were enjoying the moment. Then I looked at him chewing on his pipe, and was suddenly deeply moved. I had to say what was in my heart. It took a lot of nerve for me to speak up because he was so reserved.

I said, "I just want to thank you for being my father. I think you're the greatest man I ever met and I love you."

He smiled slowly before he said,

"Yes, son, that's very nice."

"Dad, I'd like to hear you say it, too."

"What?"

"Do you like me?"

"Well, I love you."

"Then let me hear it." And he did.

Three weeks later he was gone.

—JOHN RITTER

His heritage to his children wasn't words or possessions, but an unspoken treasure, the treasure of his example as a man and a father. More than anything I have, I'm trying to pass that on to my children.

—WILL ROGERS

Life with Father

THERE WAS A TIME in my boyhood when I felt that Father had handicapped me severely in life by naming me after him, "Clarence." All literature, so far as I could see, was thronged with objectionable persons named Clarence. Percy was bad enough, but there had been some good fighters named Percy. The only Clarence in history was a duke who did something dirty at Tewkesbury, and who died a ridiculous death afterwards in a barrel of malmsey.

As for the Clarences in the fiction I read, they were horrible. In one story, for instance, there were two brothers, Clarence and Frank. Clarence was a "vain, disagreeable little fellow," who was proud of his curly hair and fine clothes, while Frank was a "rollicking boy who was ready to play games with anybody." Clarence didn't like to play games, of course. He just minced around looking on.

One day when the mother of these boys had gone out, this story went on, Clarence "tempted" Frank to disobey her and fly their kite on the roof. Frank didn't want to, but Clarence kept taunting him and daring him until Frank was stung into doing it. After the two boys went up to the roof, Frank got good and dirty, running up and down and stumbling over scuttles, while Clarence sat there, giving him orders, and kept his natty clothes tidy. To my horror, he even spread out his handkerchief on the trapdoor to sit on. And to crown all, this sneak told on Frank as soon as their mother came in.

This wasn't an exceptionally mean Clarence, either. He was just run-of-the-mill. Some were worse.

So far as I could ever learn, however, Father had never heard of these stories, and had never dreamed of there being anything objectionable in his name. Quite the contrary. And yet as a boy he had lived a good rough-and-tumble boy's life. He had played and fought on the city streets, and kept a dog in Grandpa's stable, and stolen rides to Greenpoint Ferry on the high, lurching bus. In the summer he had gone to West Springfield and had run down Shad Lane through the trees to the house where Grandpa was born, and had gone barefoot and driven the cows home just as though he had been named Tom or Bill.

He had the same character as a boy, I suppose, that he had as a man, and he was too independent to care if people thought his name fancy. He paid no attention to the prejudices of others, except to disapprove of them. He had plenty of prejudices himself, of course, but they were his own. He was humorous and confident and level-headed, and I imagine that if any boy had tried to make fun of him for being named

Clarence, Father would simply have laughed and told him he didn't know what he was talking about.

I asked Mother how this name had ever happened to spring up in our family. She explained that my great-great-grandfather was Benjamin Day, and my great-grandfather was Henry, and consequently my grandfather had been named Benjamin Henry. He in turn had named his eldest son Henry and his second son Benjamin. The result was that when Father was born there was no family name left. The privilege of choosing a name for Father had thereupon been given to Grandma, and unluckily for the Day family she had been reading a novel, the hero of which was named Clarence.

I knew that Grandma, though very like Grandpa in some respects, had a dreamy side which he hadn't, a side that she usually kept to herself, in her serene, quiet way. Her romantic choice of this name probably made Grandpa smile, but he was a detached sort of man who didn't take small matters seriously, and who drew a good deal of private amusement from the happenings of everyday life. Besides, he was partly to blame in this case, because that novel was one he had published himself in his magazine.

I asked Mother, when she had finished, why I had been named Clarence too.

It hadn't been her choice, Mother said. She had suggested all sorts of names to Father, but there seemed to be something wrong with each one. When she had at last spoken of naming me after him, however, he had said at once that that was the best suggestion yet—he said it sounded just right.

Father and I would have had plenty of friction in any case. This identity of names made things worse. Every time that I had been more of a fool than he liked, Father would try to impress on me my responsibilities as his eldest son, and above all as the son to whom he had given his name, as he put it. A great deal was expected, it seemed to me, of a boy who was named after his father. I used to envy my brothers, who didn't have anything expected of them on this score at all.

I envied them still more after I was old enough to begin getting letters. I then discovered that when Father "gave" me his name he had also, not unnaturally, I had to admit, retained it himself, and when anything came for Clarence S. Day he opened it, though it was sometimes for me.

He also opened everything that came addressed to Clarence S. Day, Jr. He didn't do this intentionally, but unless the "Jr." was clearly written, it looked like "Esq.," and anyhow Father was too accustomed to open all Clarence Day letters to remember about looking carefully every time for a "Jr." So far as mail and express went, I had no name at all of my own.

For the most part nobody wrote to me when I was a small boy except firms whose advertisements I had read in the *Youth's Companion* and to whom I had written requesting them to send me their circulars. These circulars described remarkable bargains in magicians' card outfits, stamps and coins, pocket knives, trick spiders, and imitation fried eggs, and they seemed interesting and valuable to me when I got them. The trouble was that Father usually got them and at once tore them up. I then had to write for such circulars again, and if Father got the second one too, he would sometimes explode with annoyance. He became particularly indignant one year, I remember, when he was repeatedly urged to take advantage of a special bargain sale of false whiskers. He said that he couldn't understand why these offerings kept pouring in. I knew why, in this case, but at other times I was often surprised myself at the number he got, not realizing that as a result of my postcard request my or our name had been automatically put on several large general mailing lists.

During this period I got more of my mail out of Father's wastebasket than I did from the postman.

At the age of twelve or thirteen, I stopped writing for these childish things and turned to a new field. Father and I, whichever of us got at the mail first, then began to receive not merely circulars but personal letters beginning:

DEAR FRIEND DAY:
In reply to your valued request for one of our Mammoth Agents' Outfits, kindly forward postoffice order for $1.49 to cover cost of postage and packing, and we will put you in a position to earn a large income in your spare time with absolutely no labor on your part, by taking subscriptions for *The Secret Handbook of Mesmerism,* and our *Tales of Blood* series.

And one spring, I remember, as the result of what I had intended to be a secret application on my part, Father was assigned "the exclusive rights for Staten Island and Hoboken of selling the Gem Home Popper for Pop Corn. Housewives buy it at sight."

After Father had stormily endured these afflictions for a while, he and I began to get letters from girls. Fortunately for our feelings, these were rare, but they were ordeals for both of us. Father had forgotten, if he ever knew, how silly young girls can sound, and I got my first lesson in how unsystematic they were. No matter how private and playful they meant their letters to be, they forgot to put "Jr." on the envelope every once in so often. When Father opened these letters, he read them all the way through, sometimes twice, muttering to himself over and over: "This is very peculiar. I don't understand this at all. Here's a letter to me from some person I never heard of. I can't see what it's about." By the time it had occurred to him that possibly the letter might be for me, I was red and embarrassed and even angrier at the girl than at Father. And on days when he had read some of the phrases aloud to the family, it nearly killed me to claim it.

Lots of fellows whom I knew had been named after their fathers without having such troubles. But although Father couldn't have been kinder-hearted or had any better intentions, when he saw his name on a package or envelope it never dawned on him that it might not be for him. He was too active in his habits to wait until I had a chance to get at it. And as he was also single-minded and prompt to attend to unfinished business, he opened everything automatically and then did his best to dispose of it.

This went on even after I grew up, until I had a home of my own. Father was always perfectly decent about it, but he never changed. When he saw I felt sulky, he was genuinely sorry and said so, but he couldn't see why all this should annoy me, and he was surprised and amused that it did. I used to get angry once in a while when something came for me which I particularly hadn't wished him to see and which I would find lying, opened, on the hall table marked "For Jr.?" when I came in; but nobody could stay angry with Father—he was too utterly guiltless of having meant to offend.

He often got angry himself, but it was mostly at things, not at persons, and he didn't mind a bit (as a rule) when persons got angry at him. He even declared, when I got back from college, feeling dignified, and told him that I wished he'd be more careful, that he suffered from these mistakes more than I did. It wasn't *his* fault, he pointed out, if my stupid correspondents couldn't remember my name, and it wasn't any pleasure to him to be upset at his breakfast by finding that a damned lunatic company in Battle Creek had sent him a box of dry bread crumbs, with a letter asserting that this rubbish would be good for his stomach. "I admit I threw it into the fireplace,

Clarence, but what else could I do? If you valued this preposterous concoction, my dear boy, I'm sorry. I'll buy another box for you today, if you'll tell me where I can get it. Don't feel badly! I'll buy you a barrel. Only I hope you won't eat it."

In the days when Mrs. Pankhurst and her friends were chaining themselves to lamp-posts in London, in their campaign for the vote, a letter came from Frances Hand trustfully asking "Dear Clarence" to do something to help Woman Suffrage— speak at a meeting, I think. Father got read in the face. "Speak at one of their meet- ings!" he roared at Mother. "I'd like nothing better! You can tell Mrs. Hand that it would give me great pleasure to inform all those crackpots in petticoats exactly what I think of their antics."

"Now, Clare," Mother said, "you mustn't talk that way. I like that nice Mrs. Hand, and anyhow this letter must be for Clarence."

One time I asked Father for his opinion of a low-priced stock I'd been watching. His opinion was that it was not worth a damn. I thought this over, but I still wished to buy it, so I placed a scale order with another firm instead of with Father's office, and said nothing about it. At the end of the month this other firm sent me a statement, set- ting forth each of my little transactions in full, and of course they forgot to put the "Jr." at the end of my name. When Father opened the envelope, he thought at first in his excitement that this firm had actually opened an account for him without being asked. I found him telling Mother that he'd like to wring their damned necks.

"That must be for me, Father," I said, when I took in what had happened.

We looked at each other.

"You bought this stuff?" he said incredulously. "After all I said about it?"

"Yes, Father."

He handed over the statement and walked out of the room.

Both he and I felt offended and angry. We stayed so for several days, too, but we then made it up.

Once in a while when I got a letter that I had no time to answer I used to address an envelope to the sender and then put anything in it that happened to by lying around on my desk—a circular about books, a piece of newspaper, an old laundry bill—anything at all, just to be amiable, and yet at the same time to save myself the trouble of writing. I happened to tell several people about this private habit of mine at a dinner one night—a dinner at which Alice Duer Miller and one or two other writers were present. A little later she wrote me a criticism of Henry James and ended by saying that I needn't send her any of my old laundry bills because she wouldn't stand it. And she forgot to put on the "Jr."

"In the name of God," Father said bleakly, "this is the worst yet. Here's a woman who says I'd better not read *The Golden Bowl,* which I have no intention whatever of doing, and she also warns me for some unknown reason not to send her my laundry bills."

The good part of all these experiences, as I realize now, was that in the end they drew Father and me closer together. My brothers had only chance battles with him. I had a war. Neither he nor I relished its clashes, but they made us surprisingly intimate.

A Boy and His Dad

A boy and his dad on a fishing trip—
There is a glorious fellowship!
Father and son and the open sky
And the white clouds lazily drifting by,
And the laughing stream as it runs along
With the clicking reel like a martial song,
And the father teaching the youngster gay
How to land a fish in the sportsman's way.

Which is happier, man or boy?
The soul of the father is steeped in joy,
For he's finding out, to his heart's delight,
That his son is fit for the future fight.
He is learning the glorious depths of him,
And the thoughts he thinks and his every whim,
And he shall discover, when night comes on,
How close he has grown to his little son.

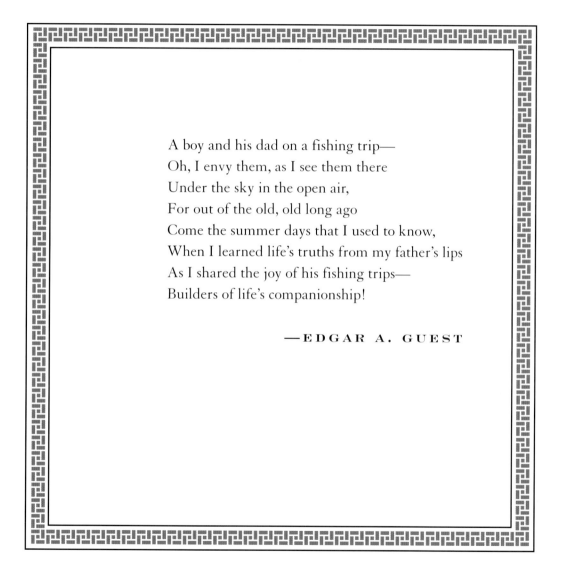

A boy and his dad on a fishing trip—
Oh, I envy them, as I see them there
Under the sky in the open air,
For out of the old, old long ago
Come the summer days that I used to know,
When I learned life's truths from my father's lips
As I shared the joy of his fishing trips—
Builders of life's companionship!

—EDGAR A. GUEST

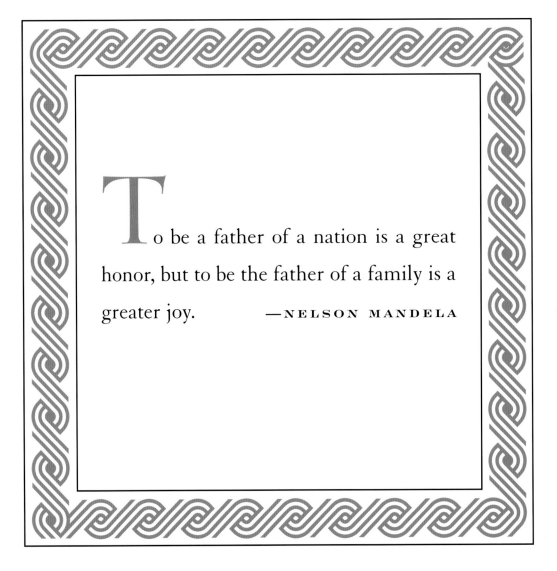

To be a father of a nation is a great honor, but to be the father of a family is a greater joy. —NELSON MANDELA

An Hour Before Daylight

BY JIMMY CARTER

LATE ONE AFTERNOON when I was about ten, Daddy asked me to keep his fish while he walked down the river to talk to some of his friends. I tied his stringer with mine on the belt loop on my down-stream side while I continued fishing, enjoying the steady pull of the current on our day's catch. It wasn't long before I watched my cork move slowly and steadily up under a snag and knew I had a big one. After a few minutes I saw the copperhead, the largest fish of the day. As I struggled with the sharply bent cane pole, I wondered how I was going to hold the fish while untying the two stringers. Then a cold chill went down my spine as I realized that the tugging of the current on the stringers was gone, as were all our fish! My belt loop had broken.

I threw my pole up on the nearest sandbar, forgot the hooked fish, and began to dive madly into the river below where I had been standing. Then I heard Daddy's voice calling me:

"Hot," he said, "what's wrong?"

"I've lost the fish, Daddy."

"All of them? Mine, too?"

"Yes, sir." I began to cry, even as I continued diving, and the tears and water ran down my face together each time I came up for breath.

Daddy was rarely patient with foolishness or mistakes, but, after a long silence, he said, "Let them go, Hot. There are a lot more fish in the river. We'll get them tomorrow."

I almost worshipped him.

Emile

*B*UT BUSINESS, OFFICIAL CARES, duties, you say! Duties indeed! the last, doubtless, is that of a father! Let us not think it strange that a man whose wife disdains to nourish the fruit of their union himself disdains to undertake its education. There is no more charming picture than that of a family life; but the lack of one trait disfigures all the others. If the mother has too little strength to be a nurse, the father will have too much business to be a teacher. The children sent from home and dispersed in boarding-schools, convents, and colleges, will carry otherwheres the love of home—or, rather, they will bring home the habit of being attached to nothing. Brothers and sisters will scarcely know one another. When they are all assembled in state, they can be very polite and formal, and will treat each other as strangers. The moment that intimacy between parents ceases, the moment that family intercourse no longer gives sweetness to life, it becomes at once necessary to resort to lower pleasures in order to supply what is lacking. Where is the man so stupid as not to see the logic of all this?

A father who merely feeds and clothes the children he has begotten so far fulfills but a third of his task. To the races, he owes men; to society, men of social dispositions; and to the state, citizens. Every man who can pay this triple debt and does not pay it, is guilty of a crime, and the more guilty, perhaps, when the debit is only half paid. He who can not fulfill the duties of a father has no right to become such. Neither poverty, nor business, nor fear of the world, can excuse him from the duty of supporting and educating his own children. Reader, believe me when I predict that whoever has a heart and neglects such sacred duties will long shed bitter tears over his mistake, and will never find consolation for it.

Simon's Papa

BY GUY DE MAUPASSANT

*N*OON HAD JUST STRUCK. The school-door opened and the youngsters streamed out tumbling over one another in their haste to get out quickly. But instead of promptly dispersing and going home to dinner as was their daily wont, they stopped a few paces off, broke up into knots and set to whispering.

The fact was that that morning Simon, the son of La Blanchotte, had, for the first time, attended school.

They had all of them in their families heard of La Blanchotte; and although in public she was welcome enough, the mothers among themselves treated her with compassion of a somewhat disdainful kind, which the children had caught without in the least knowing why.

As for Simon himself, they did not know him, for he never went abroad, and did not play around with them through the streets of the village or along the banks of the river. So they loved him but little; and it was with a certain delight, mingled with astonishment, that they gathered in groups this morning, repeating to each other this sentence, concocted by a lad of fourteen or fifteen who appeared to know all about it, so sagaciously did he wink: "You know Simon—well, he has no papa."

La Blanchotte's son appeared in his turn upon the threshold of the school.

He was seven or eight years old, rather pale, very neat, with a timid and almost awkward manner.

He was making his way back to his mother's house when the various groups of his schoolfellows, perpetually whispering, and watching him with the mischievous and heartless eyes of children bent upon playing a nasty trick, gradually surrounded him and ended by inclosing him altogether. There he stood amid them, surprised and embarrassed, not understanding what they were going to do with him. But the lad who had brought the news, puffed up with the success he had met with, demanded:

"What do you call yourself?"

He answered: "Simon."

"Simon what?" retorted the other.

The child, altogether bewildered, repeated: "Simon."

The lad shouted at him: "You must be named Simon something! That is not a name—Simon indeed!"

And he, on the brink of tears, replied for the third time:

"I am named Simon."

The urchins began laughing. The lad triumphantly lifted up his voice: "You can see plainly that he has no papa."

A deep silence ensued. The children were dumfounded by this extraordinary, impossibly monstrous thing—a boy who had not a papa; they looked upon him as a phenomenon, an unnatural being, and they felt rising in them the hitherto inexplicably pity of their mothers for La Blanchotte. As for Simon, he had propped himself against a tree to avoid falling, and he stood there as if paralyzed by an irreparable disaster. He sought to explain, but he could think of no answer for them, no way to deny this horrible charge that he had no papa. At last he shouted at them quite recklessly: "Yes, I have one."

"Where is he?" demanded the boy.

Simon was silent, he did not know. The children shrieked, tremendously excited. These sons of toil, nearly related to animals, experienced the cruel craving which makes the fowls of a farmyard destroy one of their own kind as soon as it is wounded. Simon suddenly spied a little neighbor, the son of a widow, whom he had always seen, as he himself was to be seen, quite alone with his mother.

"And no more have you," he said, "no more have you a papa."

"Yes," replied the other, "I have one."

"Where is he?" rejoined Simon.

"He is dead," declared the brat with superb dignity, "he is in the cemetery, is my papa."

A murmur of approval rose amid the scapegraces, as if the fact of possessing a papa dead in a cemetery made their comrade big enough to crush the other one who had no papa at all. And these rogues, whose fathers were for the most part evildoers, drunkards, thieves, and ill-treaters of their wives hustled each other as they pressed closer and closer to Simon as though they, the legitimate ones, would stifle in their pressure one who was beyond the law.

The lad next to Simon suddenly put his tongue out at him with a waggish air and shouted at him:

"No papa! No papa!"

Simon seized him by the hair with both hands and set to work to demolish his legs with kicks, while he bit his cheek ferociously. A tremendous struggle ensued between the two boys, and Simon found himself beaten, torn, bruised, rolled on the ground in the middle of the ring of applauding little vagabonds. As he arose, mechanically brushing his little blouse all covered with dust with his hand, some one shouted at him:

"Go and tell your papa."

He then felt a great sinking in his heart. They were stronger than he, they had beaten him and he had no answer to give them, for he knew it was true that he had no papa. Full of pride he tried for some moments to struggle against the tears which were suffocating him. He had a choking fit, and then without cries he began to weep with great sobs which shook him incessantly. Then a ferocious joy broke out among his enemies, and just like savages in fearful festivals, they took one another by the hand and danced in a circle about him as they repeated in refrain:

"No papa! No papa!"

But suddenly Simon ceased sobbing. Frenzy overtook him. There were stones under his feet; he picked them up and with all his strength hurled them at his tormentors. Two or three were struck and ran away yelling, and so formidable did he appear that the rest became panic-stricken. Cowards, like a jeering crowd in the presence of an exasperated man, they broke up and fled. Left alone, the little thing without a father set off running toward the fields, for a recollection had been awakened which nerved his soul to a great determination. He made up his mind to drown himself in the river.

He remembered, in fact, that eight days ago a poor devil who begged for his livelihood had thrown himself into the water because he had no more money. Simon had been there when they fished him out again; and the sight of the fellow, who had seemed to him so miserable and ugly, had then impressed him—his pale cheeks, his long drenched beard, and his open eyes being full of calm. The bystanders had said:

"He is dead."

And some one had added:

"He is quite happy now."

So Simon wished to drown himself also because he had no father, just as the wretched being did who had no money.

He reached the water and watched it flowing. Some fishes were rising briskly in the clear stream and occasionally made little leaps and caught the flies on the surface. He stopped crying in order to watch them, for their feeding interested him vastly. But, at intervals, as in the lulls of a tempest, when tremendous gusts of wind snap off trees and then die away, this thought would return to him with intense pain:

"I am about to drown myself because I have no papa."

It was very warm and fine weather. The pleasant sunshine warmed the grass; the water shone like a mirror; and Simon enjoyed for some minutes the happiness of that languor which follows weeping, desirous even of falling asleep there upon the grass in the warmth of noon.

A little green frog leaped from under his feet. He endeavored to catch it. It escaped him. He pursued it and lost it three times following. At last he caught it by one of its hind legs and began to laugh as he saw the efforts the creature made to escape. It gathered itself up on its large legs and then with a violent spring suddenly stretched them out as stiff as two bars.

Its eyes stared wide open in their round, golden circle, and it beat the air with its front limbs, using them as though they were hands. It reminded him of a toy made with straight slips of wood nailed zigzag one on the other, which by a similar movement regulated the exercise of the little soldiers fastened thereon. Then he thought of his home and of his mother, and overcome by great sorrow he again began to weep. His limbs trembled; and he placed himself on his knees and said his prayers as before going to bed. But he was unable to finish them, for such hurried and violent sobs overtook him that he was completely overwhelmed. He thought no more, he no longer heeded anything around him but was wholly given up to tears.

Suddenly a heavy hand was placed upon his shoulder, and a rough voice asked him:

"What is it that causes you so much grief, my fine fellow?"

Simon turned round. A tall workman, with a black beard and hair all curled, was staring at him good-naturedly. He answered with his eyes and throat full of tears:

"They have beaten me because—I—I have no papa—no papa."

"What!" said the man smiling, "why, everybody has one."

The child answered painfully amid his spasms of grief:

"But I—I—I have none."

Then the workman became serious. He had recognized La Blanchotte's son, and although a recent arrival to the neighborhood he had a vague idea of her history.

"Well," said he, "console yourself, my boy, and come with me home to your mother. She will give you a papa."

And so they started on the way, the big one holding the little one by the hand. The man smiled afresh, for he was not sorry to see this Blanchotte, who by popular report was one of the prettiest girls in the country-side—and, perhaps, he said to himself, at the bottom of his heart, that a lass who had erred once might very well err again.

They arrived in front of a very neat little white house.

"There it is," exclaimed the child, and he cried: "Mamma."

A woman appeared, and the workman instantly left off smiling, for he at once perceived that there was no more fooling to be done with the tall pale girl, who stood austerely at her door as though to defend from one man the threshold of that house where she had already been betrayed by another. Intimidated, his cap in his hand, he stammered out:

"See, Madame, I have brought you back your little boy, who had lost himself near the river."

But Simon flung his arms about his mother's neck and told her, as he again began to cry:

"No, mamma, I wished to drown myself, because the others had beaten me—had beaten me—because I have no papa."

A burning redness covered the young woman's cheeks, and, hurt to the quick, she embraced her child passionately, while the tears coursed down her face. The man, much moved, stood there, not knowing how to get away. But Simon suddenly ran to him and said:

"Will you be my papa?"

A deep silence ensued. La Blanchotte, dumb and tortured with shame, leaned against the wall, her hands upon her heart. The child, seeing that no answer was made him, replied:

"If you do not wish it, I shall return to drown myself."

The workman took the matter as a jest and answered laughing:

"Why, yes, I wish it certainly."

"What is your name, then," went on the child, "so that I may tell the others when they wish to know your name?"

"Philip," answered the man.

Simon was silent a moment so that he might get the name well into his memory; then he stretched out his arms, quite consoled, and said:

"Well, then, Philip, you are my papa."

The workman, lifting him from the ground, kissed him hastily on both cheeks, and then strode away quickly.

When the child returned to school next day he was received with a spiteful laugh, and at the end of school, when the lads were on the point of recommencing, Simon threw these words at their heads as he would have done a stone: "He is named Philip, my papa."

Yells of delight burst out from all sides.

"Philip who? Philip what? What on earth is Philip? Where did you pick up your Philip?"

Simon answered nothing; and immovable in faith he defied them with his eye, ready to be martyred rather than fly before them. The schoolmaster came to his rescue and he returned home to his mother.

For a space of three months, the tall workman, Philip, frequently passed by La Blanchotte's house, and sometimes made bold to speak to her when he saw her sewing near the window. She answered him civilly, always sedately, never joking with him, nor permitting him to enter her house. Notwithstanding this, being like all men, a bit of a coxcomb, he imagined that she was often rosier than usual when she chatted with him.

But a fallen reputation is so difficult to recover, and always remains so fragile that, in spite of the shy reserve La Blanchotte maintained, they already gossiped in the neighborhood.

As for Simon, he loved his new papa much, and walked with him nearly every evening when the day's work was done. He went regularly to school and mixed in a dignified way with his schoolfellows without ever answering them back. One day, however, the lad who had first attacked him said to him:

"You have lied. You have not a papa named Philip."

"Why do you say that?" demanded Simon, much disturbed.

The youth rubbed his hands. He replied:

"Because if you had one he would be your mamma's husband."

Simon was confused by the truth of this reasoning; nevertheless he retorted:

"He is my papa all the same."

"That can very well be," exclaimed the urchin with a sneer, "but that is not being your papa altogether."

La Blanchotte's little one bowed his head and went off dreaming in the direction of the forge belonging to old Loizon, where Philip worked.

This forge was entombed in trees. It was very dark there, the red glare of a formidable furnace alone lit up with great flashes five blacksmiths, who hammered upon their anvils with a terrible din. Standing enveloped in flame, they worked like demons, their eyes fixed on the red-hot iron they were pounding; and their dull ideas rising and falling with their hammers.

Simon entered without being noticed and quietly plucked his friend by the sleeve. Philip turned round. All at once the work came to a standstill and the men looked on very attentively. Then, in the midst of this unaccustomed silence, rose the little slender pipe of Simon:

"Philip, explain to me what the lad at La Michande has just told me, that you are not altogether my papa."

"And why that?" asked the smith.

The child replied in all innocence:

"Because you are not my mamma's husband."

No one laughed. Philip remained standing, leaning his forehead upon the back of his great hands, which held the handle of his hammer upright upon the anvil. He mused. His four companions watched him, and, like a tiny mite among these giants, Simon anxiously waited. Suddenly, one of the smiths, voicing the sentiment of all, said to Philip:

"All the same La Blanchotte is a good and honest girl, stalwart and steady in spite of her misfortune, and one who would make a worthy wife for an honest man."

"That is true," remarked the three others.

The smith continued:

"Is it the girl's fault if she has fallen? She had been promised marriage, and I know more than one who is much respected today and has sinned every bit as much."

"That is true," responded the three men in chorus.

He resumed:

"How hard she has toiled, poor thing, to educate her lad all alone, and how much she has wept since she no longer goes out, save to church, God only knows."

"That also is true," said the others.

Then no more was heard save the roar of the bellows which fanned the fire of the furnace. Philip hastily bent himself down to Simon:

"Go and tell your mamma that I shall come to speak to her."

Then he pushed the child out by the shoulders. He returned to his work and in unison the five hammers again fell upon their anvils. Thus they wrought the iron until nightfall, strong, powerful, happy, like Vulcans satisfied. But as the great bell of a cathedral resounds upon feast days above the jingling of the other bells, so Philip's hammer, dominating the noise of the others, clanged second after second with a deafening uproar. His eye on the fire, he plied his trade vigorously, erect amid the sparks.

The sky was full of stars as he knocked at La Blanchotte's door. He had his Sunday blouse on, a fresh shirt, and his beard was trimmed. The young woman showed herself upon the threshold and said in a grieved tone:

"It is ill to come thus when night has fallen, Mr. Philip."

He wished to answer, but stammered and stood confused before her.

She resumed:

"And you understand quite well that it will not do that I should be talked about any more."

Then he said all at once:

"What does that matter to me, if you will be my wife!"

No voice replied to him, but he believed that he heard in the shadow of the room the sound of a body falling. He entered very quickly; and Simon, who had gone to his bed, distinguished the sound of a kiss and some words that his mother said very softly. Then he suddenly found himself lifted up by the hands of his friend, who, holding him at the length of his herculean arms, exclaimed to him:

"You will tell your schoolfellows that your papa is Philip Remy, the blacksmith, and that he will pull the ears of all who do you any harm."

On the morrow, when the school was full and lessons were about to begin, little Simon stood up quite pale with trembling lips:

"My papa," said he in a clear voice, "is Philip Remy, the blacksmith, and he has promised to box the ears of all who do me any harm."

This time no one laughed any longer, for he was very well known, was Philip Remy, the blacksmith, and he was a papa of whom anyone in the world would be proud.

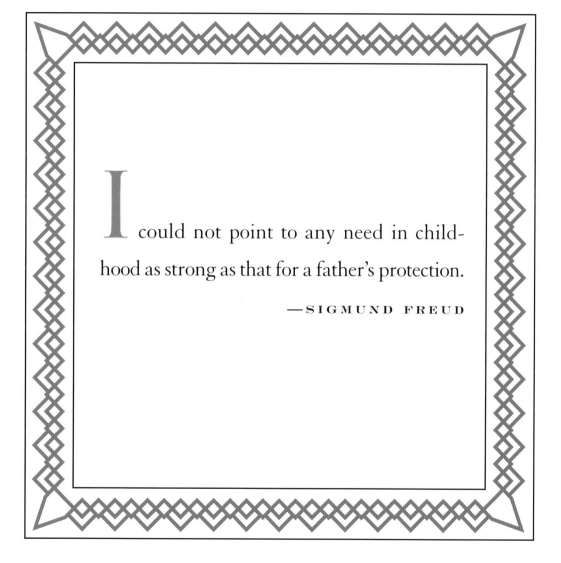

I could not point to any need in child-hood as strong as that for a father's protection.

—SIGMUND FREUD

My Son the Murderer

BY BERNARD MALAMUD

H E WAKES TO A FEELING his father is in the hallway, listening. Listening to what? Listening to him sleep and dream. To get him up and fumble for his pants. To him not going to the kitchen to eat. Staring with shut eyes in the mirror. Sitting an hour on the toilet. Flipping the pages of a book he can't read. To his rage, anguish, loneliness. The father stands in the hall. The son hears him listen.

My son the stranger, he tells me nothing.

I open the door and see my father in the hall.

Why are you standing there, why don't you go to work?

I took my vacation in the winter instead of the summer like I usually do.

What the hell for if you spend it in this dark smelly hallway watching my every move. Guessing what you don't see. What are you spying on me?

My father goes to his room and after a while comes out in the hallway again, listening.

I hear him sometimes in his room but he don't talk to me and I don't know what's what. It's a terrible feeling for a father. Maybe someday he'll write me a nice letter, my dear father. . . .

My dear son Harry, open up your door.

My son the prisoner.

My wife leaves in the morning to be with my married daughter who is having her fourth child. The mother cooks and cleans for her and takes care of the children. My daughter is having a bad pregnancy, with high blood pressure, and is in bed most of the time. My wife is gone all day. She knows something is wrong with Harry. Since he graduated college last summer he is nervous, alone, in his own thoughts. If you talk to him, half the time he yells. He reads the papers, smokes, stays in his room. Once in a while he goes for a walk.

How was the walk, Harry?

A walk.

My wife told him to go look for work and a few times he went, but when he got some kind of offer he didn't take the job.

It's not that I don't want to work. It's that I feel bad.

Why do you feel bad?

I feel what I feel. I feel what is.

Is it your health, sonny? Maybe you ought to go to a doctor?

Don't call me by that name. It's not my health. Whatever it is I don't want to talk about it. The work wasn't the kind I want.

So take something temporary in the meantime, she said.

He starts to yell. Everything is temporary. Why should I add more to what is already temporary? My guts feel temporary. The world is temporary. On top of that I don't want temporary work. I want the opposite of temporary, but where do you look for it? Where do you find it?

My father temporarily listens in the kitchen.

My temporary son.

She said I'd feel better if I work. I deny it. I'm twenty-two, since last December, a college graduate and you know where you can stick that. At night I watch the news broadcasts. I watch the war from day to day. It's a large war on a small screen. I sometimes lean over and touch the war with the flat of my hand. I'm waiting for my hand to die.

My son with the dead hand.

I expect to be drafted any day but it doesn't bother me so much anymore. I won't go. I'll go to Canada or somewhere, though the idea is a burden to me.

The way he is frightens my wife and she is glad to go off to my daughter's house in the morning to take care of the three children. I'm left alone, but he don't talk to me.

You ought to call up Harry and talk to him, my wife says to my daughter.

I will sometimes, but don't forget there's nine years' difference between our ages. I think he thinks of me as another mother around and one is enough. I used to like him, but it's hard to deal with a person who won't reciprocate.

She's got high blood pressure. I think she's afraid to call.

I took two weeks off from work. I'm a clerk at the stamps window in the Post Office. I told the superintendent I wasn't feeling so good, which is no lie, and he said I should take sick leave, but I said I wasn't that sick. I told my friend Moe Berk I was staying out because Harry had me worried.

I know what you mean, Leo. I got my own worries and anxieties about my kids. If you have two girls growing up you got hostages to fortune. Still in all, we got to live. Will you come to poker Friday night? Don't deprive yourself of a good form of relaxation.

I'll see how I feel by then, how it's coming. I can't promise.

Try to come. These things all pass away. If it looks better to you, come on over. Even if it don't look so good, come on over anyway because it might relieve the tension and worry that you're under. It's not good for your heart at your age if you carry that much worry around.

This is the worst kind of worry. If I worry about myself I know what the worry is. What I mean, there's no mystery. I can say to myself, Leo, you're a fool, stop worrying over nothing—over what, a few bucks? Over my health that always stood up pretty good although I've had my ups and downs? Over that I'm now close to sixty and not getting any younger? Everybody that don't die by the age fifty-nine gets to be sixty. You can't beat time if it's crawling after you. But if the worry is about somebody else, that's the worst kind. That's the real worry because if he won't tell you, you can't get inside the other person and find out why. You don't know where's the switch to turn off. All you can do is worry more.

So I wait in the hallway.

Harry, don't worry about the war.

Don't tell me what to worry about.

Harry, your father loves you. When you were a little boy, every night when I came home you used to run to me. I picked you up and lifted you to the ceiling. You liked to touch it with your small hand.

I don't want to hear about that anymore. It's the very thing I don't want to hear about. I don't want to hear about when I was a child.

Harry, we live like strangers. All I'm saying is I remember better days. I remember when we weren't afraid to show we loved each other.

He says nothing.

Let me cook you an egg.

I don't want an egg. It's the last thing in the world I want.

So what do you want?

He put his coat on. He pulled his hat off the clothes tree and went downstairs into the street. Harry walked along Ocean Parkway in his long coat and creased brown hat. He knew his father was following him and it filled him with rage.

He didn't turn around. He walked at a fast pace up the broad avenue. In the old days there was a bridle path at the side of the walk where the concrete bicycle path was now. And there were fewer trees now, their black branches cutting the sunless sky. At the corner of Avenue X, just about where you begin to smell Coney Island, he crossed over and began to walk home. He pretended not to see his father cross over, although he was still infuriated. The father crossed over and followed his son home. When he got to his house he figured Harry was already upstairs. He was in his room with the door shut. Whatever he did in his room he was already doing.

Leo took out his key and opened the mailbox. There were three letters. He looked to see if one of them was, by any chance, from his son to him. My dear father, let me explain myself. The reason I act as I do is. . . . But there was no such letter. One of the letters was from The Post Office Clerks Benevolence Society, which he put in his coat pocket. The other two letters were for his son. One was from the draft board. He brought it up to his son's room, knocked on the door and waited.

He waited for a while.

To the boy's grunt he said, there is a draft board letter for you. He turned the knob and entered the room. Harry was lying on the bed with his eyes shut.

You can leave it on the table.

Why don't you open it? Do you want me to open it for you?

No, I don't want you to open it. Leave it on the table.

I know what's in it.

What's in it?

That's my business.

The father left it on the table.

The other letter to his son he took into the kitchen, shut the door and boiled up some water in a kettle. He thought he would read it quickly and then seal it carefully with a little paste so that none leaked over the edge of the flap, then go downstairs and put it back in the mailbox. His wife would take it out with her key when she returned from their daughter's house and bring it up to Harry.

The father read the letter. It was a short letter from a girl. The girl said Harry had borrowed two of her books more than six months ago and since she valued them highly she would like him to send them back to her. Could he do that as soon as possible so that she wouldn't have to write again?

As Leo was reading the girl's letter Harry came into the kitchen and when he saw the surprised and guilty look on his father's face, he tore the letter out of his hands.

I ought to kill you the way you spy on me.

Leo turned away, looking out of the small kitchen window into the dark apartment-house courtyard. His face was mottled red, his eyes dull, and he felt sick.

Harry read the letter at a glance and tore it up. He then tore up the envelope marked personal.

If you do this again don't be surprised if I kill you. I'm sick of you spying on me. Harry left the house.

Leo went into his room and looked around. He looked in the dresser drawers and found nothing unusual. On the desk by the window was a paper Harry had written on. It said: Dear Edith, why don't you go fuck yourself? If you write another such letter I'll murder you.

The father got his hat and coat and left the house. He ran for a while, running then walking, until he saw Harry on the other side of the street. He followed him a half block behind.

He followed Harry to Coney Island Avenue and was in time to see him board a trolleybus going toward the Island. Leo had to wait for the next bus. He thought of taking a taxi and following the bus, but no taxi came by. The next bus came by fifteen minutes later and he took it all the way to the Island. It was February and Coney Island was cold and deserted. There were few cars on Surf Avenue and few people on the streets. It looked like snow. Leo walked on the boardwalk, amid snow flurries, looking for his son. The gray sunless beaches were empty. The hot-dog stands, shooting galleries, and bathhouses were shuttered up. The gunmetal ocean, moving like melted lead, looked freezing. There was a wind off the water and it worked its way into his clothes so that he shivered as he walked. The wind white-capped the leaden waves and the slow surf broke on the deserted beaches with a quiet roar.

He walked in the blow almost to Sea Gate, searching for his son, and then walked back. On his way toward Brighton he saw a man on the beach standing in the foaming surf. Leo went down the boardwalk stairs and onto the ribbed-sand beach. The man on the shore was Harry standing in the water up to his ankles.

Leo ran to his son. Harry, it was my mistake, excuse me. I'm sorry I opened your letter. Harry did not turn. He stayed in the water, his eyes on the leaden waves.

Harry, I'm frightened. Tell me what's the matter. My son, have mercy on me.

It's not my kind of world, Harry thought. It fills me with terror.

He said nothing.

A blast of wind lifted his father's hat off his head and carried it away over the beach. It looked as if it were going to land in the surf but then the wind blew it toward the boardwalk, rolling like a wheel along the ground. Leo chased after his hat. He chased it one way, then another, then toward the water. The wind blew the hat against his legs and he caught it. He pulled the freezing hat down tight on his head until it bent his ears. By now he was crying. Breathless, he wiped his eyes with icy fingers and returned to his son at the edge of the water.

He is a lonely man. This is the type he is, Leo thought. He will always be lonely. My son who became a lonely man.

Harry, what can I say to you? All I can say to you is who says life is easy? Since when? It wasn't for me and it isn't for you. It's life, what more can I say? But if a person don't want to live what can he do if he's dead? If he doesn't want to live maybe he deserves to die.

Come home, Harry, he said. It's cold here. You'll catch a cold with your feet in the water.

Harry stood motionless and after a while his father left. As he was leaving, the wind plucked his hat off his head and sent it rolling along the sand.

My father stands in the hallway. I catch him reading my letter. He follows me at a distance in the street. We meet at the edge of the water. He is running after his hat.

My son stands with his feet in the ocean.

From Father, with Love

BY DORIS KEARNS GOODWIN

*T*HE GAME OF BASEBALL has always been linked in my mind with the mystic texture of childhood, with the sounds and smells of summer nights and with the memories of my father.

My love for baseball was born on the first day my father took me to Ebbets Field in Brooklyn. Riding in the trolley car, he seemed as excited as I was, and he never stopped talking; now describing for me the street in Brooklyn where he had grown up, now recalling the first game he had been taken to by his own father, now recapturing for me his favorite memories from the Dodgers of his youth—the Dodgers of Casey Stengel, Zack Wheat, and Jimmy Johnston.

In the evenings, when my dad came home from work, we would sit together on our porch and relive the events of that afternoon's game which I had so carefully preserved in the large, red scorebook I'd been given for my seventh birthday. I can still remember how proud I was to have mastered all those strange and wonderful symbols that permitted me to recapture, in miniature form, the every movement of Jackie Robinson and Pee Wee Reese, Duke Snider, and Gil Hodges. But the real power of that scorebook lay in the responsibility it entailed. For all through my childhood, my father kept from me the knowledge that the daily papers printed daily box scores, allowing me to believe that without my personal renderings of all those games he missed while he was at work, he would be unable to follow our team in the only proper way a team should be followed, day by day, inning by inning. In other words, without me, his love for baseball would be forever incomplete.

To be sure, there were risks involved in making a commitment as boundless as mine. For me, as for all too many Brooklyn fans, the presiding memory of "the boys of summer" was the memory of the final playoff game in 1951 against the Giants. Going into the ninth, the Dodgers held a 4–1 lead. Then came two singles and a double, placing the winning run at the plate with Bobby Thomson at bat. As Dressen replaced Erskine with Branca, my older sister, with maddening foresight, predicted the forever famous Thomson homer—a prediction that left me so angry with her, imagining that with her words she had somehow brought it about, that I would not speak to her for days.

So the seasons of my childhood passed until that miserable summer when the Dodgers were taken away to Los Angeles by the unforgivable O'Malley, leaving all our rash hopes and dreams of glory behind. And then came a summer of still deeper sadness when my father died. Suddenly my feelings for baseball seemed an aspect of my departing youth, along with my childhood freckles and my favorite childhood haunts, to be left behind when I went away to college and never came back.

Then one September day, having settled into teaching at Harvard, I agreed, half reluctantly, to go to Fenway Park. There it was again: the cozy ballfield scaled to human dimensions so that every word of encouragement and every scornful yell could be heard on the field; the fervent crowd that could, with equal passion, curse a player for today's failures after cheering his heroics the day before; the team that always seemed to break your heart in the last week of the season. It took only a matter of minutes before I found myself directing all my old intensities toward my new team—the Boston Red Sox.

I am often teased by my women friends about my obsession, but just as often, in the most unexpected places—in academic conferences, in literary discussions, at the most elegant dinner parties—I find other women just as crazily committed to baseball as I am, and the discovery creates an instant bond between us. All at once we are deep in conversation, mingling together the past and the present, as if the history of the Red Sox had been our history too.

There we stand, one moment recollecting the unparalleled performance of Yaz in '67, the next sharing ideas on how the present lineup should be changed; one moment recapturing the splendid career of "the Splendid Splinter," the next complaining about the manager's decision to pull the pitcher the night before. And then, invariably, comes the most vivid memory of all, the frozen image of Carlton Fisk as he rounded first in the sixth game of the '75 World Series, an image as intense in its evocation of triumph as the image of Ralph Branca weeping in the dugout is in its portrayal of heartache.

There is another, more personal memory associated with Carlton Fisk, for he was, after all the years I had followed baseball, the first player I actually met in person. Apparently, he had read the biography I had written on Lyndon Johnson and wanted to meet me. Yet when the meeting took place, I found myself reduced to the shyness of childhood. There I was, a professor at Harvard, accustomed to speaking with presidents of the United States, and yet, standing beside this young man in a baseball uniform, I was speechless.

Finally Fisk said that it must have been an awesome experience to work with a man of such immense power as President Johnson—and with that, I was at last able to stammer out, with a laugh, "Not as awesome as the thought that I am really standing here talking with you."

Perhaps I have circled back to my childhood, but if this is so, I am certain that my journey through time is connected in some fundamental way to the fact that I am now a parent myself, anxious to share with my three sons the same ritual I once shared with my father.

For in this linkage between the generations rests the magic of baseball, a game that has defied the ravages of modern life, a game that is still played today by the same basic rules and at the same pace as it was played one hundred years ago. There is something deeply satisfying in the knowledge of this continuity.

And there is something else as well which I have experienced sitting in Fenway Park with my small boys on a warm summer's day. If I close my eyes against the sun, all at once I am back at Ebbets Field, a young girl once more in the presence of my father, watching the players of my youth on the grassy field below. There is magic in this moment, for when I open my eyes and see my sons in the place where my father once sat, I feel an invisible bond between our three generations, an anchor of loyalty linking my sons to the grandfather whose face they never saw but whose person they have already come to know through this most timeless of all sports, the game of baseball.

Shooting Dad

BY SARAH VOWELL

*I*F YOU WERE PASSING BY THE HOUSE where I grew up during my teenage years and it happened to be before Election Day, you wouldn't have needed to come inside to see that it was a house divided. You could have looked at the Democratic campaign poster in the upstairs window and the Republican one in the downstairs window and seen our home for the Civil War battleground it was. I'm not saying who was the Democrat or who was the Republican—my father or I—but I will tell you that I have never subscribed to *Guns & Ammo*, that I did not plaster the family vehicle with National Rifle Association stickers, and that hunter's orange was never my color.

About the only thing my father and I agreed on is the Constitution, though I'm partial to the First Amendment, while he's always favored the Second.

I am a gunsmith's daughter. I like to call my parents' house, located on a quiet residential street in Bozeman, Montana, the United States of Firearms. Guns were everywhere: the so-called pretty ones like the circa 1850 walnut muzzleloader hanging on the wall. Dad's clients' fixer-uppers leaning into corners, an entire rack right next to the TV. I had to move revolvers out of my way to make room for a bowl of Rice Krispies on the kitchen table.

I was eleven when we moved into that Bozeman house. We had never lived in town before, and this was a college town at that. We came from Oklahoma—a dusty little Muskogee County nowhere called Braggs. My parents' property there included an orchard, a horse pasture, and a couple of acres of woods. I knew our lives had changed one morning not long after we moved to Montana when, during breakfast, my father heard a noise and jumped out of his chair. Grabbing a BB gun, he rushed out the front door. Standing in the yard, he started shooting at crows. My mother sprinted after him screaming, "Pat, you might ought to check, but I don't think they do that up here!" From the look on his face, she might as well have told him that his American citizenship had been revoked. He shook his head, mumbling, "Why, shooting crows is a national pastime, like baseball and apple pie." Personally, I preferred baseball and apple pie. I looked up at those crows flying away and thought, I'm going to like it here.

Dad and I started bickering in earnest when I was fourteen, after the 1984 Democratic National Convention. I was so excited when Walter Mondale chose Geraldine Ferraro as his running mate that I taped the front page of the newspaper with her picture on it to the refrigerator door. But there was some sort of mysterious gravity surge in the kitchen. Somehow, that picture ended up in the trash all the way across the room.

Nowadays, I giggle when Dad calls me on Election Day to cheerfully inform me that he has once again canceled out my vote, but I was not always so mature. There were times when I found the fact that he was a gunsmith horrifying. And just *weird*. All he ever cared about were guns. All I ever cared about was art. There were years and years when he hid out by himself in the garage making rifle barrels and I holed up in my room reading Allen Ginsberg poems, and we were incapable of having a conversation that didn't end in an argument.

Our house was partitioned off into territories. While the kitchen and living room were well within the DMZ, the respective work spaces governed by my father and me were jealously guarded totalitarian states in which each of us declared ourselves dictator. Dad's shop was a messy disaster area, a labyrinth of lathes. Its walls were hung with the mounted antlers of deer he'd bagged, forming a makeshift museum of death. The available flat surfaces were buried under a million scraps of paper on which he sketched his mechanical inventions in blue ball-point pen. And the floor, carpeted with spiky metal shavings, was a tetanus shot waiting to happen. My domain was the cramped, cold space known as the music room. It was also a messy disaster area, an obstacle course of musical instruments—piano, trumpet, baritone horn, valve trombone, various percussion doodads (bells!), and recorders. A framed portrait of the French composer Claude debussy was nailed to the wall. The available flat surfaces were buried under piles of staff paper, on which I penciled in the pompous orchestra music given titles like "Prelude to the Green Door" (named after an O. Henry short story by the way, not the watershed porn flick *Behind the Green Door*) I starting writing in junior high.

It has been my experience that in order to impress potential suitors, skip the teen debussy anecdotes and stick with the always attention-getting line "My dad makes guns." Though it won't cause the guy to like me any better, it will make him handle the inevitable breakup with diplomacy—just in case I happen to have any loaded family heirlooms lying around the house.

But the fact is, I have only shot a gun once and once was plenty. My twin sister, Amy, and I were six years old—six—when Dad decided that it was high time we learned how to shoot. Amy remembers the day he handed us the gun for the first time differently. She liked it.

Amy shared our father's enthusiasm for firearms and the quick-draw cowboy mythology surrounding them. I tended to daydream through Dad's activities—the car trip to Dodge City's Boot Hill, his beloved John Wayne Westerns on TV. My sister, on the other hand, turned into Rooster Cogburn Jr., devouring Duke movies with Dad. In fact, she named her teddy bear Duke, hung a colossal John Wayne portrait next to her bed, and took to wearing one of those John Wayne shirts that button on the side. So when Dad led us out to the backyard when we were six and, to Amy's delight, put the gun in her hand, she says she felt it meant that Daddy trusted us and that he thought of us as "big girls."

But I remember holding the pistol only made me feel small. It was so heavy in my hand. I stretched out my arm and pointed it away and winced. It was a very long time before I had the nerve to pull the trigger and I was so scared I had to close my eyes. It felt like it just went off by itself, as if I had no say in the matter, as if the gun just had this *need*. The sound it made was as big as God. It kicked little me back to the ground like a bully, like a foe. It hurt. I don't know if I dropped it or just handed it back over to my dad, but I do know that I never wanted to touch another one again. And, because I believed in the devil, I did what my mother told me to do every time I felt an evil presence. I looked at the smoke and whispered under my breath, "Satan, I rebuke thee."

It's not like I'm saying I was traumatized. It's more like I was decided. Guns: Not For Me. Luckily, both my parents grew up in exasperating households where children were considered puppets and/or slaves. My mom and dad were hell-bent on letting my sister and me make our own choices. So if I decided that I didn't want my father's little death sticks to kick me to the ground again, that was fine with him. He would go hunting with my sister, who started calling herself "the loneliest twin in history" because of my reluctance to engage in family activities.

Of course, the fact that I was allowed to voice my opinions did not mean that my father would silence his own. Some things were said during the Reagan administration that cannot be taken back. Let's just say that I blamed Dad for nuclear proliferation and Contra aid. He believed that if I had my way, all the guns would be confiscated and it would take the commies about fifteen minutes to parachute in and assume control.

We're older now, my dad and I. The older I get, the more I'm interested in becoming a better daughter. First on my list: Figure out the whole gun thing.

Not long ago, my dad finished his most elaborate tool of death yet. A cannon. He built a nineteenth-century cannon. From scratch. It took two years.

My father's cannon is a smaller replica of a cannon called the Big Horn Gun in front of Bozeman's Pioneer Museum. The barrel of the original has been filled with concrete ever since some high school kids in the '50s pointed it at the school across the street and shot out its windows one night as a prank. According to Dad's historical source, a man known to scholars as A Guy at the Museum, the cannon was brought to Bozeman around 1870, and was used by local white merchants to fire at the Sioux and Cheyenne Indians who blocked their trade access to the East in 1874.

"Bozeman was founded on greed," Dad says. The courthouse cannon, he continues, "definitely killed Indians. The merchants filled it full of nuts, bolts, and chopped-up horseshoes. Sitting Bull could have been part of those engagements. They definitely ticked off the Indians, because a couple of years later, Custer wanders into them at Little Bighorn. The Bozeman merchants were out to cause trouble. They left fresh baked bread with cyanide in it on the trail to poison a few Indians."

Because my father's sarcastic American history yarns rarely go on for long before he trots out some nefarious ancestor of ours—I come from a long line of moonshiners, Confederate soldiers, murderers, even Democrats—he cracks that the merchants hired some "community-minded Southern soldiers from North Texas." These soldiers had, like my great-great-grandfather John Vowell, fought under pro-slavery guerrilla William C. Quantrill. Quantrill is most famous for riding into Lawrence, Kansas, in 1863 flying a black flag and commanding his men pharaohlike to "kill every male and burn down every house."

"John Vowell," Dad says, "had a little rep for killing people." And since he abandoned my great-grandfather Charles, whose mother died giving birth to him in 1870, and wasn't seen again until 1912, Dad doesn't rule out the possibility that John Vowell could have been one of the hired guns on the Bozeman Trail. So the cannon isn't just another gun to my dad. It's a map of all his obsessions—firearms, certainly, but also American history and family history, subjects he's never bothered separating from each other.

After tooling a million guns, after inventing and building a rifle barrel boring machine, after setting up that complicated shop filled with lathes and blueing tanks and outmoded blacksmithing tools, the cannon is his most ambitious project ever. I thought that if I was ever going to understand the ballistic bee in his bonnet, this was my chance. It was the biggest gun he ever made and I could experience it and spend time with it with the added bonus of not having to actually pull a trigger myself.

I called Dad and said that I wanted to come to Montana and watch him shoot off the cannon. He was immediately suspicious. But I had never taken much interest in his work before and he would take what he could get. He loaded the cannon into the back of his truck and we drove up into the Bridger Mountains. I was a little worried that the National Forest Service would object to us lobbing fiery balls of metal onto its property. Dad laughed, assuring me that "you cannot shoot fireworks, but this is considered a fire*arm*."

It is a small cannon, about as long as a baseball bat and as wide as a coffee can. But it's heavy—110 pounds. We park near the side of the hill. Dad takes his gunpowder and other tools out of this adorable wooden box on which he has stenciled "PAT G. VOWELL CANNONWORKS." Cannonworks: So that's what NRA members call a metal-strewn garage.

Dad plunges his homemade bullets into the barrel, points it at an embankment just to be safe, and lights the fuse. When the fuse is lit, it resembles a cartoon. So does the sound, which warrants Ben Day dot words along the lines of *ker-pow!* There's so much Fourth of July smoke everywhere I feel compelled to sing the national anthem.

I've given this a lot of thought—how to convey the giddiness I felt when the cannon shot off. But there isn't a sophisticated way to say this. It's just really, really cool. My dad thought so, too.

Sometimes, I put together stories about the more eccentric corners of the American experience for the public radio. So I happen to have my tape recorder with me, and I've never seen levels like these. Every time the cannon goes off, the delicate needles which keep track of the sound quality lurch into the bad, red zone so fast and so hard I'm surprised they don't break.

The cannon was so loud and so painful, I had to touch my head to make sure my skull hadn't cracked open. One thing that my dad and I share is that we're both a little hard of hearing—me from Aerosmith, him from gunsmith.

He lights the fuse again. The bullet knocks over the log he was aiming at. I instantly utter a sentence I never in my entire life thought I would say. I tell him, "Good shot, Dad."

Just as I'm wondering what's coming over me, two hikers walk by. Apparently, they have never seen a man set off a homemade cannon in the middle of the wilderness while his daughter holds a foot-long microphone up into the air recording its terrorist boom. One hiker gives me a puzzled look and asks, "So you work for the radio and that's your dad?"

Dad shoots the cannon again so that they can see how it works. The other hiker says, "That's quite the machine you got there." But he isn't talking about the cannon. He's talking about my tape recorder and my microphone—which is called a *shotgun* mike. I stare back at him, then I look over at my father's cannon, then down at my microphone, and I think, Oh. My. God. My dad and I are the same person. We're both smart-alecky loners with goofy projects and weird equipment. And since this whole target practice outing was my idea, I was no longer his adversary. I was his accomplice. What's worse, I was liking it.

I haven't changed my mind about guns. I can get behind the cannon because it is a completely ceremonial object. It's unwieldy and impractical, just like everything else I care about. Try to rob a convenience store with this 110-pound Saturday night special, you'd still be dragging it in the door Sunday afternoon.

I love noise. As a music fan, I'm always waiting for that moment in a song when something just flies out of it and explodes in the air. My dad is a one-man garage band, the kind of rock'n'roller who slaves away at his art for no reason other than to make his own sound. My dad is an artist—a pretty driven, idiosyncratic one, too. He's got his last *Gesamtkunstwerk* planned out. It's a performance piece. We're all in it—my mom, the loneliest twin in history, and me.

When my father dies, take a wild guess what he wants done with his ashes. Here's a hint: It requires a cannon.

"You guys are going to love this," he smirks, eyeballing the cannon. "You get to drag this thing up on top of the Gravellies on opening day of hunting season. And looking off at Sphinx Mountain, you get to put me in little paper bags. I can take my last hunting trip on opening morning."

I'll do it, too. I will have my father's body burned into ashes. I will pack these ashes into paper bags. I will go to the mountains with my mother, my sister, and the cannon. I will plunge his remains into the barrel and point it into a hill so that he doesn't take anyone with him. I will light the fuse. But I will not cover my ears. Because when I blow what used to be my dad into the earth, I want it to hurt.

PART III

Fatherly
Advice and
Guidance

I have found that the best way to give advice to your children is to find out what they want and then advise them to do it.

—HARRY S. TRUMAN

Charles Dickens

1868

I NEED NOT TELL YOU that I love you dearly, and am very, very sorry in my heart to part with you. But this life is half made up of partings, and these pains must be borne. It is my comfort and my sincere conviction that you are going to try the life for which you are best fitted. I think its freedom and wildness more suited to you than any experiment in a study or office would ever have been, and without that training, you could have followed no other occupation. . . .

Never take a mean advantage of anyone in any transaction, and never be hard upon people who are in your power. Try to do to others, as you would have them do for you, and do not be discouraged if they fail sometimes. It is much better for you that they should fail in obeying the greatest rule laid down by our Saviour, than that you should. . . .

Only one more thing on this head. The more we are in earnest as to feeling it, the less we are disposed to hold forth about it. Never abandon the wholesome practice of saying your own private prayers, night and morning. I have never abandoned it myself, and I know the comfort of it.

I hope you will always be able to say in life, that you had a kind father.

Thomas Jefferson

1783

THE ACQUIREMENTS WHICH I hope you will make under the tutors I have provided for you will render you more worthy of my love, and if they cannot increase it they will prevent its diminution. Consider the good lady who has taken you under her roof, who has undertaken to see that you perform all your exercises, and to admonish you in all those wanderings from what is right or what is clever to which your inexperience would expose you, consider her I say as your mother, as the only person to whom, since the loss with which heaven has been pleased to afflict you, you can now look up; and that her displeasure or disapprobation on any occasion will be an immense misfortune which should you be so unhappy as to incur by any unguarded act, think no concession too much to regain her good will. With respect to the distribution of your time the following is what I should approve.

from 8. to 10 o'clock practise music.

from 10. to 1. dance one day and draw another

from 1. to 2. draw on the day you dance, and write a letter the next day.

from 3. to 4. read French.

from 4. to 5. exercise yourself in music.

from 5. till bedtime read English, write &c.

Strive to be good under every situation and to all living creatures, and to acquire those accomplishments which I have put in your power, and which will go far towards ensuring you the warmest love of your affectionate father.

P.S. Keep my letters and read them at times that you may always have present in your mind those things which will endear you to me.

F. Scott Fitzgerald

DEAR PIE: 1933

I feel very strongly about your doing duty. Would you give me a little more documentation about your reading in French? I am glad you are happy—but I never believe much in happiness. I never believe in misery either. Those are things you see on the stage or the screen or the printed page, they never really happen to you in life.

All I believe in in life is the rewards for virtue (according to your talents) and the *punishments* for not fulfilling your duties, which are doubly costly. If there is such a volume in the camp library, will you ask Mrs. Tyson to let you look up a sonnet of Shakespeare's in which the line occurs *Lilies that fester smell far worse than weeds.*

Have had no thoughts today, life seems composed of getting up a *Saturday Evening Post* story. I think of you, and always pleasantly; but if you call me "Pappy" again I am going to take the White Cat out and beat his bottom *hard, six times for every time you are impertinent.* Do you react to that?

I will arrange the camp bill.

Half-wit, I will conclude. Things to worry about:

Worry about courage

Worry about cleanliness

Worry about efficiency

Worry about horsemanship . . .

Things not to worry about:

Don't worry about popular opinion

Don't worry about dolls

Don't worry about the past

Don't worry about the future

Don't worry about growing up

Don't worry about anybody getting ahead of you

Don't worry about triumph

Don't worry about failure unless it comes through your own fault

Don't worry about mosquitoes

Don't worry about flies

Don't worry about insects in general

Don't worry about parents

Don't worry about boys

Don't worry about disappointments

Don't worry about pleasures

Don't worry about satisfactions

Things to think about:

What am I really aiming at?

How good am I in comparison to my contemporaries in regard to:

(a) Scholarship

(b) Do I really understand about people and am I able to get along with them?

(c) Am I trying to make my body a useful instrument or am I neglecting it?

With dearest love

Bronson Alcott

1839

THIS IS YOUR BIRTHDAY. You have now lived eight years with your father and mother, six years with your loving sister Louisa, and almost four years with your sweet little sister Elizabeth. Your father knows how much you love him. . . . He wants to see his little girl kind and gentle, and sweet-tempered, as fragrant as the flowers in springtime, and as beautiful as they are when the dew glitters on them in the morning dew.

Do you want to know how you can be so beautiful and sweet? It is easy. Only try, with all your resolution, to mind what that silent teacher in your breast says to you: that is all.

A birthday is a good time to begin anew: throwing away the old habits, as you would old clothes, and never putting them on again. Begin, my daughter, today, and when your next birthday shall come, how glad you will be that you made the resolution. Resolution makes all things new. . . .

When you were a few weeks old, you smiled on us. I sometimes see that same look and the same smile on your face, and feel that my daughter is yet good and pure. O keep it there, my daughter, and never lose it.

Ogden Nash

D EAREST ISABEL,
I gather that by now you have decided Mr. X is too old for you, as well as being a very silly man, but I am not pleased by the episode and I trust that by now you aren't either. The propensity of old men for flirting with young girls has been the object of coarse merriment since primeval days, as I should think your reading, if nothing else, should have told you.

You should be intelligent enough to know that in various eras of history it has been fashionable to laugh at morals, but the fact of the matter is that Old Man Morals just keeps rolling along and the laughers end up as driftwood on a sandbar. You can't beat the game, because morals as we know them represent the sum of the experience of the race. That is why it distressed me to find you glibly tossing off references to divorce. You surely have seen enough of its effects on your friends to know that it is a tragic thing even when forced on one partner by the vices of the other.

Read the marriage vows again—they are not just words, not even just a poetic promise to God. They are a practical promise to yourself to be happy. This I know from simply looking around me.

It bothers me to think that you may have sloppy—not sophisticated but sloppy—ideas about life. I have never tried to blind you to any side of life, through any form of censorship, trusting in your intelligence to learn of, and to recognize, evil without approving or participating in it. So please throw Iris March and all the golden doomed Bohemian girls away and be Isabel—there's more fun in it for you.

Keep on having your gay time, but just keep yourself in hand, and remember that generally speaking it's better to call older men Mister.

I love you tremendously,
Daddy

LETTER FROM

Leopold Mozart

TO HIS SON

WOLFGANG AMADEUS

MY SON! You are hot-tempered and impulsive in all your ways!
Since your childhood and boyhood your whole character has changed. As a child and
a boy you were serious rather than childish, and when you sat at the clavier or were
otherwise intent on music, no one dared to make the slightest jest. Why, even your
expression was so solemn that, observing the early efflorescence of your talent and
your ever grave and thoughtful little face, many discerning people of different coun-
tries sadly doubted whether your life would be a long one. But now, as far as I can see,
you are much too ready to retort in a bantering tone to the first challenge—and that,
of course, is the first step towards undue familiarity, which anyone who wants to pre-
serve his self-respect will try to avoid in this world. A goodhearted fellow is inclined,

it is true, to express himself freely and naturally; nonetheless it is a mistake to do so. And it is just your good heart which prevents you from detecting any shortcomings in a person who showers praises on you, has a great opinion of you and flatters you to the skies, and who makes you give him all your confidence and affection; whereas as a boy you were so extraordinarily modest that you used to weep when people praised you overmuch. The greatest art of all is *to know oneself* and then, my dear son, to do as I do, that is *to endeavour to get to know others through and through.* This, as you know, has always been my study; and certainly it is a fine, useful and indeed most necessary one.

Sir Thomas More

1517?

*I*T IS NOT SO STRANGE that I love you with my whole heart, for being a father is not a tie which can be ignored. Nature in her wisdom has attached the parent to the child and bound them spiritually together with a Herculean knot. This tie is the source of my consideration for your immature minds, a consideration which causes me to take you often into my arms. This tie is the reason why I regularly fed you cake and gave you ripe apples and pears. This tie is the reason why I used to dress you in silken garments and why I never could endure to hear you cry. You know, for example, how often I kissed you, how seldom I whipped you. My whip was invariably a peacock's tail. Even this I wielded hesitantly and gently so that sorry welts might not disfigure your tender seats. Brutal and unworthy to be called father is he who does not weep himself at the tears of his child. How other fathers act I do not know, but you know well how gentle and devoted is my manner towards you, for I have always profoundly loved my own children and I have always been an indulgent parent—as every father ought to be. But at this moment my love has increased so much that it seems to me I used not to love you at all. This feeling of mine is produced by your adult manners, adult despite your tender years; by your instincts, trained in noble principles which must be learned; by your pleasant way of speaking, fashioned for clarity; and by your very careful weighing of every word. These characteristics of yours so strangely tug at my heart, so closely bind me to you, my children, that my being your father (the only reason for many a father's love) is hardly a reason at all for my love of you. Therefore, most dearly beloved children all, continue to endear yourselves to your father and, by those same accomplishments which make me think that I had not loved you before, make me think hereafter (for you can do it) that I do not love you now.

Theodore Roosevelt

White House, Oct. 2, 1903.

DEAR KERMIT:

I was very glad to get your letter. Am glad you are playing football. I should be very sorry to see either you or Ted devoting most of your attention to athletics, and I haven't got any special ambition to see you shine overmuch in athletics at college, at least (if you go there), because I think it tends to take up too much time; but I do like to feel that you are manly and able to hold your own in rough, hardy sports. I would rather have a boy of mine stand high in his studies than high in athletics, but I could a great deal rather have him show true manliness of character than show either intellectual or physical prowess; and I believe you and Ted both bid fair to develop just such character.

There! you will think this a dreadfully preaching letter! I suppose I have a natural tendency to preach just at present because I am overwhelmed with my work. I enjoy being President, and I like to do the work and have my hand on the lever. But it is very worrying and puzzling, and I have to make up my mind to accept every kind of attack and misrepresentation. It is a great comfort to me to read the life and letters of Abraham Lincoln. I am more and more impressed every day, not only with the man's wonderful power and sagacity, but with his literally endless patience, and at the same time his unflinching resolution.

White House, April 1, 1906.

Darling Quenty-Quee:

Slipper and the kittens are doing finely. I think the kittens will be big enough for you to pet and have some satisfaction out of when you get home, although they will be pretty young still. I miss you all dreadfully, and the house feels big and lonely and full of echoes with nobody but me in it; and I do not hear any small scamps running up and down the hall just as hard as they can; or hear their voices while I am dressing; or suddenly look out through the windows of the office at the tennis ground and see them racing over it or playing in the sand-box. I love you very much.

PART IV

Favorite Recipes for Dad

Super Bowl Nacho Dip

1 8-ounce container of cream cheese
1 can refried beans
2 cups sharp cheddar cheese, shredded
1 handful black olives, sliced

1 scallion, sliced
1 1/2 cups salsa
tortilla chips

1. Spread softened cream cheese in bottom of a pie plate.
2. Layer refried beans on top of cream cheese.
3 Spread salsa over refried beans.
4. Cover top with shredded cheese.
5. Sprinkle olives and scallions on top.
6. Bake in 325°F oven for about 20 minutes until bubbly. Serve with tortilla chips.

(Makes 4 to 6 servings)

Bourbon Dogs

*2 packages hot dogs,
cut into 1/2-inch pieces
1 cup ketchup
1 cup brown sugar
1 cup bourbon*

*1 cup water
1 onion, chopped
1 tablespoon butter
1 teaspoon olive oil*

1. Sauté onion in butter and olive oil until pearly.
2. Add remaining ingredients and cover.
3. Simmer over medium flame, stirring occasionally,
   for approximately two hours (until sauce thickens).

(Makes 6 to 8 servings)

Baked Clams

12 little-neck clam shells
6 ½-ounce can chopped clams in juice
1 cup Italian bread crumbs
⅓ cup olive oil
1 clove garlic, finely chopped

1. Mix bread crumbs with olive oil until moistened.
2. Add garlic.
3. Place clam shells on a cookie sheet and fill with chopped clams and clam juice.
4. Mound bread crumb mixture on top.
5. Add enough water to cover bottom of cookie sheet, along with a pinch of olive oil and any leftover bread crumbs.
6. Preheat oven to 350°F for 5 to 10 minutes and bake clams for approximately 25 to 30 minutes or until breadcrumbs are lightly browned.

(Makes 4 servings)

Grilled Swordfish

2 to 3 pounds swordfish, 1-inch thick   1 clove garlic, minced

4 tablespoons peanut oil   4 bay leaves

2 tablespoons olive oil   1 teaspoon paprika

2 tablespoons lemon juice   1 teaspoon salt

1 tablespoon lime juice   ground pepper to taste

2 tablespoons white wine

1. Combine all ingredients (except swordfish) in flat tray.
2. Add swordfish and cover.
3. Marinade at least 3 to 4 hours, preferably overnight.
4. Preheat grill. Lightly spray grill with nonstick vegetable oil spray.
5. Grill 8 minutes on each side on medium direct heat until no longer pink. Should be white, but still juicy.

(Makes 4 servings)

Maryland Crab Cakes

3 cans crabmeat *1 tablespoon fresh parsley, chopped*
$1/2$ cup bread crumbs *2 teaspoons Worcestershire sauce*
1 egg, beaten *$1/4$ teaspoon salt*
1 teaspoon dijon mustard *$1/4$ teaspoon white pepper*
5 tablespoons mayonnaise *$1/4$ cup oil*

1. Combine all ingredients except crabmeat. Mix well.
2. Pour mixture over well-drained crabmeat and fold in gently and thoroughly.
3. Heat enough oil to cover bottom of fry pan.
4. Shape into 6 cakes and fry until golden brown, turning once after 2 to 3 minutes.
NOTE: 12 mini-crab cakes can also be made for appetizers.

(Makes 6 servings)

Linguini & Clam Sauce

1 1/2 dozen fresh clams (If fresh clams not available, use 1 can minced clams.)

4 cloves garlic, chopped

1/2 teaspoon lemon rind, grated

1 teaspoon corn starch

1 tablespoon fresh parsley, chopped

1 bottle clam juice

1/2 teaspoon oregano

2 bay leaves

1/2 cup white wine

2 tablespoons olive oil

1 pound linguini or thin spaghetti

salt and pepper to taste

2 tablespoons grated Romano or Parmesan cheese

1. Clean and mince the clams saving the juice. Strain through a handkerchief several times to remove sand.
2. Sauté garlic in olive oil.
3. Add fresh and bottled clam juice along with oregano, bay leaves, white wine, lemon rind, and cornstarch.
4. Cook together for approximately 10 minutes on low flame.
5. Add clams and bring to a boil. Cook for 1 minute.
6. Cook pasta according to package directions. Toss together with clam sauce.
7. Add salt and pepper to taste. Top with parsley and grated cheese.

(Makes 4 servings)

Barbecued Pork Spare Ribs

1 rack baby-back pork ribs   1 ¹/₂ tablespoons onion powder
1 ¹/₂ tablespoons garlic powder   1 tablespoon seasoned salt
1 ¹/₂ tablespoons paprika   ¹/₂ cup barbecue sauce

1. Rinse ribs and remove membrane from the back using sharp knife. Pat dry.
2. Combine all dry ingredients and rub generously on the ribs.
3. Cover and refrigerate for at least 2 hours.
4. Grill ribs on low indirect heat for 2 hours.
5. During the last 20 minutes brush on barbecue sauce. Turning the ribs, baste several times while still on the grill. Detach ribs with a sharp knife.

(Makes 4 servings)

Firehouse Chicken

4 1-inch thick chicken cutlets   1 egg, beaten
2 tablespoons flour   1 ½ sticks butter
2 tablespoons plain bread crumbs   ½ cup hot sauce
1 teaspoon seasoned salt

1. Combine dry ingredients in a plastic bag.
2. Dip chicken into egg.
3. Place chicken in bread-crumb bag and shake to coat.
4. Place 2 to 3 tablespoons of butter into frying pan and brown chicken for
   3 to 4 minutes on each side or until light brown in color.
5. Place chicken into baking dish. Cover with foil and bake at 350°F for 20 minutes.
6. Add 1 stick melted butter and ¾ cup hot sauce.
7. Pour mixture over chicken and continue to bake for 15 to 20 minutes uncovered.

N O T E : Hot sauce may be increased to taste.

(Makes 4 servings)

Beer & Bratwurst

1 pound bratwurst   *1 medium onion, sliced*
12 ounces of beer   *10 whole black peppercorns*

1. In large saucepan combine all ingredients. Cook until almost boiling.
2. Cover and simmer for 10 minutes.
3. Remove bratwurst. Continue to simmer onions until tender.
4. Broil or grill bratwurst 3 to 5 inches from heat about 3 to 5 minutes on each side.
5. Drain onions and place on top of bratwurst to serve.

(Makes 4 servings)

Stick-To-Your-Ribs Beef Stew

1 ½ to 2 pounds beef stew meat cut into 1-inch cubes
¼ cup and 2 tablespoons flour
2 teaspoons salt
¼ teaspoon pepper
3 tablespoons oil
2 stalks celery, cut into pieces
2 medium onions, quartered
2 beef bouillon cubes
1 bay leaf
2 ¼ cups water
1 8-ounce can of tomato sauce
6 carrots, cut into pieces
4 medium potatoes, cut into pieces

1. Coat meat with mixture of ¼ cup flour, salt and pepper.
2. Brown meat in hot oil.
3. Add celery, onions, bouillon cubes, bay leaf, 2 cups water and tomato sauce.
4. Cover and simmer for 1 ½ hours or until meat is tender.
5. Remove bay leaf. Add carrots and potatoes.
6. Cover and continue to cook for 30 to 35 minutes or until vegetables are tender. Add more water if necessary.
7. Combine 2 tablespoons flour and ¼ cup water in small bowl. Add to stew. Cook until mixture thickens and boils.

(Makes 4 to 6 servings)

Zesty Corned Beef & Cabbage

4 to 5 pounds of corned beef

6 to 8 carrots, peeled and cut in half

6 medium potatoes, peeled and quartered

1 medium head of cabbage, quartered

1 package of dry onion-soup mix

1. Place beef in large pot with enough cold water to cover.
2. Bring to boil and add onion-soup mix.
3. Lower heat. Cook till beef is tender (approximately 2 hours).
4. Add carrots and potatoes. Cook for 30 minutes.
5. Add cabbage and cook for additional 25 minutes.

(Makes 6 to 8 servings)

German Potato Salad

2 pounds potatoes

1 pound bacon sliced across in strips

1 medium onion, diced

4 tablespoons brown sugar

4 tablespoons vinegar

2 tablespoons cornstarch

$^1/_2$ cup cold water

salt and pepper to taste

1. Peel and cut potatoes into $^1/_4$-inch slices.
2. Fill large frying pan with water and salt. Add potatoes and cook until soft.
4. Drain potatoes leaving some water in the pan.
6. In a separate pan cook bacon.
7. Cook onion in bacon drippings.
8. Add vinegar and brown sugar. Cook until brown sugar dissolves.
9. Add cornstarch mixed with $^1/_2$ cup of cold water.
10. Pour bacon mixture over potatoes gently tossing.
11. Add salt and pepper to taste.
12. Cook together about 5 minutes.

(Makes 8 to 10 servings)

Savory Pepper Steak

1 pound flank steak   *¹/₃ cup water*
¹/₂ cup onion, chopped   *3 tablespoons of tomato sauce*
3 green peppers, sliced   *1 tablespoon vegetable oil*
¹/₄ cup soy sauce   *cornstarch*
¹/₄ cup dry sherry

1. Brown steak over medium heat. Remove from heat.
2. Cook onions and pepper in oil until tender.
3. Add soy sauce, sherry, water, tomato sauce, and water.
4. Add steak back in and cook for additional 5 minutes. If sauce is not at desired thickness, add a tablespoon of cornstarch mixed with water.
5. Serve with rice.

(Makes 4 servings)

Hearty Meat Sauce

5 28-ounce cans of imported crushed tomatoes
2 28-ounce cans water
1 to 2 6-ounce cans tomato paste
1 pound chopped beef
1 pound sausage
6 pieces of pork neck bones
6 ounces red wine

1 large onion, chopped
5 cloves garlic, minced
$1/4$ cup olive oil
1 tablespoon oregano
$1/2$ teaspoon salt
$1/2$ teaspoon black pepper
$1/4$ teaspoon crushed red pepper

1. In a large pot, sauté chopped meat and sausage meat until brown.
2. After browning remove meat and drain in a colander.
3. Brown pork neck bones and set aside with meat.
4. Sauté onion in olive oil until translucent then add garlic for 3 minutes.
5. Add in crushed tomatoes, water, meat, pork neck bones, and wine.
6. Bring mixture to a simmer and add remaining spices.
7. Let simmer $2 1/2$ hours stirring every 10 to 15 minutes.
8. Remove pork neck bones and add 1 can tomato paste.
9. Allow simmering to continue for 30 minutes, if sauce is not at desired consistency add second can of paste and simmer for additional 30 minutes.

(Makes 10 to 12 servings)

Flank Steak Marinade

———◈———

1 1/2 to 2 pounds flank steak	1 teaspoon garlic powder
1/4 cup soy sauce	1 1/2 teaspoon ground ginger
3 tablespoons honey	3/4 cup vegetable oil
3 tablespoons cider vinegar	1 onion, finely chopped

1. Combine all ingredients. Marinade at least 4 hours (preferably overnight).

(Makes 4 servings)

Chicken Marinade

———◈———

2/3 cup vegetable oil	1 teaspoon salt
1/3 cup vinegar	1/8 teaspoon oregano
1 egg	1/8 teaspoon rosemary
1/2 cup water	1/8 teaspoon pepper
3 cloves garlic, minced	

1. Combine all ingredients and mix in blender. Marinade chicken at least 4 hours (preferably overnight).